SOCIOLOGY IN FOCUS
General Editor: Murray

Knowledge

Tomas Boronski

LONGMAN
London and New York

LONGMAN GROUP UK LIMITED
*Longman House, Burnt Mill, Harlow, Essex CM2 2JE, UK
and Associated Companies throughout the World.*

**Published in the United States of America
by Longman Inc., New York.**

© **Longman Group UK Limited 1987**
*All rights reserved; no part of this publication
may be reproduced, stored in a retrieval system,
or transmitted in any form or by any means, electronic,
mechanical, photocopying, recording, or otherwise,
without the prior written permission of the Publishers.*

First published 1987
ISBN 0 582 35564 8

Set in 10/11pt Bembo, Linotron 202

Produced by Longman Group (Far East) Limited

Printed in Hong Kong

British Library Cataloguing in Publication Data
Boronski, Tomas
    Knowledge. – (Sociology in focus series).
    1. Knowledge, Sociology of
    1. Title   II. Series
    306'.42   BD175

    ISBN 0-582-35564-8

Library of Congress Cataloging-in-Publication Data
Boronski, Tomas.
    Knowledge.

    (Sociology in focus series)
    Bibliography: p.
    Includes index.
    Summary: Examines the major sources of knowledge in
society, science, religion, and education, with the
intention of integrating the topic into a study of
sociology.
    1. Sociology – Methodology. 2. Knowledge, Sociology
of. [1. Sociology – Methodology. 2. Knowledge,
Sociology of] I. Title. II. Series.

HM66.B74   1988   306'.42   87-17017
ISBN 0-582-35564-8

Contents

To Catherine

Series introduction

Sociology in Focus aims to provide an up–to–date, coherent coverage of the main topics that arise on an introductory course in sociology. While the intention is to do justice to the intricacy and complexity of current issues in sociology, the style of writing has deliberately been kept simple. This is to ensure that the student coming to these ideas for the first time need not become lost in what can appear initially as jargon.

Each book in the series is designed to show something of the purpose of sociology and the craft of the sociologist. Throughout the different topic areas the interplay of theory, methodology and social policy have been highlighted, so that rather than sociology appearing as an unwieldy collection of facts, the student will be able to grasp something of the process whereby sociological understanding is developed. The format of the books is broadly the same throughout. Part 1 provides an overview of the topic as a whole. In Part 2 the relevant research is set in the context of the theoretical, methodological and policy issues. The student is encouraged to make his or her own assessment of the various arguments, drawing on the statistical and reference material provided both here and at the end of the book. The final part of the book contains both statistical material and a number of 'Readings'. Questions have been provided in this section to direct students to analyse the materials presented in terms of both theoretical assumptions and methodological approaches. It is intended that this format should enable students to exercise their own sociological imaginations rather than to see sociology as a collection of universally accepted facts, which just have to be learned.

While each book in the series is complete within itself, the similarity of format ensures that the series as a whole provides an integrated and balanced introduction to sociology. It is intended that the text can be used both for individual and classroom study, while the inclusion of the variety of statistical and documentary materials lend themselves to both the preparation of essays and brief seminars.

PART 1

Introduction

1 Perspectives in the sociology of knowledge

Without doubt in the Western world we live in an age of mass consumption, not only of material goods but also of knowledge and information. Never before have so many been able to exploit such vast amounts of knowledge. The education system, the media and the advanced forms of information technology make access to this knowledge ever easier. It should not be forgotten, however, that this is only a recent phenomenon, for in medieval times only a small minority were able to read and write. These were mainly the clergy who had the legal monopoly of all teaching from the university to the elementary school. G. G. Coulton (1930) estimates that only about one-tenth of the medieval population had an education of any kind and it was only in the last century that compulsory primary education was introduced in Britain.

This is not to say that there were no generally accepted beliefs and ideas in medieval society. In fact, among all social groups there exists what sociologists would call a 'world view' or '*Weltanschauung*'. This refers to a system of ideas and beliefs which serves to support the existing social order, and the sociologist of knowledge is concerned with why a particular social group has a particular '*Weltanschauung*'.

The feudal world view

It can be seen that during the feudal period in Europe the Christian world view prevailed, and from the pulpit the clergy taught ideas such as those of St Anselm:

> Is not every man to labour as a bird is to flight? Does not every man serve under the name of Lord or serf? And is not he who is called a serf in the Lord, the Lord's freeman, and he who is called free, is he not Christ's serf? So if all men labour and serve, and the serf is a freeman of the Lord, and the freeman is a serf of Christ, what does it matter apart from the sin of pride either to the world or to God who is called a serf and who is called free?

In this way the Church extolled the virtues of the institution of serfdom, and asserted that it was the door to 'spiritual freedom'. Attempts by the peasants to throw off their condition were considered an exhibition of the sin of pride. There is no doubt that despite the demise of feudalism, the Church and its teachings played a crucial role in maintaining the existing social order which endured in Europe for several hundred years.

Ideas, beliefs and knowledge, then, have tangible effects, and in the feudal period Europe was in effect governed jointly by the monarch and the Church, for without the teachings of the latter feudal kings could not have ruled for so long. The Church endowed the monarchy with divine qualities by claiming that the king had been appointed by God to rule on earth. In return the king gave the Church considerable power and land. As the clergy in feudal times was a ruling group whose ideas were considered to be true for all time, it constituted what has been called a 'theocracy'.

Definition

With regard to such world views the sociologist will be concerned with their origins and effects. They will ask *how* we know what we know and *why* we accept or share particular views of reality in preference to others. Briefly defined, then, *the sociology of knowledge is that branch of sociology which is used to examine the social origins of knowledge and the way in which individuals and social groups claim to know and believe something, despite the variety of alternative ways of seeing the world.*

The social origins of knowledge

As in other areas of sociology, there are competing views as to the origin and nature of knowledge in society. Broadly speaking, there are two main methods of approaching the problem: firstly, the *structuralist* approach represented by functionalism and certain types of Marxism; and secondly, the *interactionist* approach represented by the phenomenologists.

Structuralism

The structuralists start from the assumption that we can only understand the origin and nature of knowledge by studying the social system as a whole. Although **Marxists** and **functionalists** differ in most other respects, they claim that ideas are ultimately the result of the way in which society is organized.

DURKHEIM AND FUNCTIONALISM

For **Durkheim** the term 'society' has more than just a common-sense meaning. It is a concept which is basic to functionalist theory, and at its simplest society is compared to the result of a chemical fusion of two or more elements each contributing to the composition of an entirely new substance which has completely different characteristics from the individual elements of which it is composed. So although society is made up of individuals each with their own ideas and beliefs, together they form a single moral community. The force keeping these individuals together, according to Durkheim, is the *collective conscience*. This refers to the common ideas and beliefs held by a community and the generally accepted standards of behaviour. It stands above the individual and acts as a model for all to follow. For this reason, according to Durkheim, crimes are not just offences by one individual against another but they are an affront to the moral order and as such threaten social order. In the words of Durkheim, crime threatens the *social solidarity* of society. Sometimes the reaction to crime may, to the dispassionate observer, go beyond what might seem to be reasonable. Take the following example of the punishment prescribed by the ancient Germans for damaging a tree:

> Sacred groves were common among the ancient Germans, and tree-worship is hardly extinct amongst their descendants to the present day. How serious that worship was in former times may be gathered from the ferocious penalty appointed by the German laws for such as dared to peel the bark of a standing

tree. The culprit's navel was to be cut out and nailed to the part of the tree which he had peeled, and he was to be driven round and round the tree till all his guts were wound about its trunk.
(Sir James Frazer, *The Golden Bough*, London, Macmillan, 1974, first published 1922)

From a modern legal perspective such a punishment for damaging a tree would be unthinkable, but this is because we no longer consider trees to be holy. In ancient German society such an act threatened a collectively held sentiment – it offended against society and as such was severely punished.

Durkheim's theory of the collective conscience illustrates the importance he attaches to the collectively supported moral order. This theme appears throughout his work which concentrates on knowledge as a product of society and the role it plays in reinforcing social solidarity.

MARX AND MARXISM

Marx also recognized that there was a close relationship between ideas and society. He believed that ideas and human consciousness are the products of our material existence or the *mode of production* (as he called it). According to Marx each historical period is characterized by its own particular method of providing for the material needs of its members. For example, in ancient Greece and Rome most of the labour was performed by slaves from which the slave owners profited; in feudal society it was from the toil of serfs and peasants that the landlords derived the wealth with which to live a life of conspicuous consumption. Such systems, however, could not last for long, according to Marx, without a set of beliefs and ideas which serves to justify these social and economic relationships. Marx argued that the dominant group in each mode of production, the *ruling class*, develops just such a body of ideas which he called the 'ruling class ideology'. Because it controls the economy Marx believed that the ruling class is able to influence the way in which the other members of society think. It can convince the dominated group that its role in society and the way society divides its produce is fair.

'Ideology' is a very important term in Marxist sociology because it refers to a form of control and domination by one group over another without force. An ideology helps to justify a system of inequality and makes it seem natural. For example, the systems of slavery in ancient Greece and Rome had their own ideologies which justified a situation in which about 80 per cent of the population were slaves who did all the manual work as well as many of the bureaucratic tasks and were even artists. Their rewards for such work was just enough food and clothing to survive. But what sort of ruling class ideology existed?

> There were a few treatises, especially in the Roman period, on the best way to plant crops, the best agricultural implements to use, and the best ways to supervise, control and punish slaves. In addition, there were a large number of justifications of slavery. Even such brilliant philosophers as Plato and Aristotle argued that slavery was 'natural', was the only possible system, and would exist forever; they argued that some men and women were born to be slaves and were inherently inferior, while others were born superior and were meant to be slave owners . . . this was the dominant ideology and they simply took it for granted.
> (E. K. Hunt, *Property and Prophets: The Evolution of Economic Institutions and Ideologies*, New York, Harper and Row, 1981)

Phenomenology and the sociology of knowledge

While the structuralists see society as the source of knowledge, the phenomenologists claim that it has its origins in the way in which individuals interpret the world. They start from an examination of social interaction and the meanings which individuals attach to their exchanges with others in everyday life. By sharing common experiences people come to see the world in a particular way and, once accepted, this reality gets transmitted to a new generation and assumes the status of 'objectivity'. In other words, it is accepted as the 'truth'. According to **Alfred Schutz** societies will therefore differ in terms of their *definitions of reality*. Take, for example, the possible explanations for the causes of *misfortune*.

In Western society accidents such as car crashes or injury at work are put down to carelessness, lack of concentration or chance. In other societies explanations may be different. For example, among the Azande of the Sudan witchcraft will be held responsible:

> Azande observe clearly and generalize about the empirical 'how's' of misfortunes: a heavy weight crushes a man. . . . But they also try to explain what has been called the 'particularity'

of misfortunes – what particular persons suffer them. Here beliefs in witchcraft enter. Similarly, beliefs in witchcraft explain why one man's crops fail and not another's, why a man falls ill when he has previously been well and his fellows are still well, why a small wound festers instead of healing, why a poisonous snake bites a man so that he dies. Among the Azande the belief is also used to explain why particular warriors and not others are killed by particular enemies in battle. Clearly those slain were killed by enemy spears: but an internal enemy, the witch, has caused this particular death. And this witch is held responsible in internal tribal relations.

(Max Gluckman, *Politics, Law and Ritual in Tribal Society*, Oxford, Blackwell, 1977)

Berger and **Luckmann** (*The Social Construction of Reality*, 1976) call such a system of beliefs and explanation of reality a *universe of meaning*. This provides a way for members of society to place mysterious events within the realm of human understanding and helps to give comfort and relieve anxiety in times of crisis. A universe of meaning needs constant support and justification or, in the words of Berger and Luckmann, 'legitimation'. This is because the ideas which a society holds may come under threat from a variety of sources from both within and outside. According to Berger and Luckmann one of the most important and widespread sources of legitimation which has ever existed is religion, for it is through religion that most societies in the past have been able to place their way of life within the realm of super-natural forces. Their universe of meaning is thus provided with internal strength and cohesion. In medieval Europe, for example, men and women saw the universe as a place in which all the stars and other heavenly bodies revolved around the earth. Such ideas provided the medieval person with a sense of security in the fact that we were at the centre of God's universe. Astronomers (until Copernicus) also observed the universe in that way.

They were committed to the wheel of the heavens: the hosts of heaven must march around the earth. That had become an article of faith, as if the Church had made up its mind that the system of Ptolemy was invented not by a Levantine Greek but by the Almighty Himself.

(J. Bronowski, *The Ascent of Man*, London, BBC Publications, 1973)

THE PROBLEM OF RELATIVISM

One of the issues raised by a phenomenological theory of knowledge is that of *relativism*. A relativistic theory is one which does not provide any criteria whereby we can judge the truth or otherwise of beliefs and ideas. Relativists argue that because all knowledge is socially produced – that is, it is the product of its social context – ideas about truth and reality will vary depending upon the type of society in which they are located. One well-known proponent of this view is P. Winch ('Understanding a Primitive Society', 1964), who argues that because each society or culture has its own criteria of reality and rationality it would be a mistake to describe a particular view of the world as *right* or *wrong*. He claims that the correct way to approach the problem would be to judge it purely in terms of its own standards. Let us take as our example Winch's interpretation of witchcraft among the Azande as described by E. E. Evans-Pritchard (*Witchcraft, Oracles and Magic among the Azande of the Anglo-Egyptian Sudan*, 1937). The latter argues that by modern scientific standards witchcraft is clearly a 'bad' explanation of reality by the Azande for it cannot be 'proved' that witches exist. Evans-Pritchard concludes that the Azande do not present a picture of society based on 'objective reality'. Winch, on the other hand,

> objects to the view that Zande witchcraft does not accord with 'objective reality', on the grounds that there is no intelligible concept of reality that can be used to evaluate the truth or falsity of the belief-systems involved in every form of life or social practice.
> (R. Keat and J. Urry, *Social Theory as Science*, London, Routledge and Kegan Paul, 1975)

A major criticism of relativistic theories, however, is that since relativists argue that there are no universal standards of truth it is inconsistent for them to argue that theories based on relativism are true. In the following chapters we shall see how other sociologists try to tackle this problem.

PART 2

Origins and developments

2 Introduction

In this chapter we will look at the earliest attempts to produce a sociological explanation for the origins of knowledge. This will involve an examination of the work of the functionalist Emile Durkheim, especially his theory of how individuals in society are able to think in a collective manner and the way this contributes to social solidarity. Parson's contribution to the functionalist theory of knowledge will also be discussed. Finally, we will look at Marx's theory and in particular his use of the concept of 'ideology' as well as more recent developments in Marxist theory such as the work of Louis Althusser and Antonio Gramsci.

Durkheim and the origins of knowledge

Durkheim was a *positivist* who believed that the only way we can obtain reliable knowledge is through the scientific method, which involves the construction of a *hypothesis* – a proposition or set of propositions which can be tested – and the development of theories on the basis of the results. He claimed that society is governed by laws, just as is the world of nature, and that these laws could be measured and their effects gauged by adopting, as closely as possible, the techniques and methods of the natural sciences. For Durkheim, even in society observation and experimentation can be used to confirm or disprove a hypothesis.

Most students will be familiar with Durkheim's study of suicide, which he attempted to analyse in a scientific manner. He tried to show that there is a relationship between the degree to which individuals are integrated into society and the suicide rate.

Suicide for Durkheim, therefore, is a social phenomenon; it is the result of social forces or laws. Knowledge in society is seen in the same way, for it too is regarded as a social product which has an effect on society.

Durkheim's theory will be of interest not just to the sociologist of knowledge but also to the sociologist of religion, for he sees knowledge as the product of society in general and of religion in particular. Religion played that part in social life in the past which science and philosophy play today, for as we have seen, in feudal times religion provided the basis for defining what it is important to know and how to think.

Religion and knowledge

For Durkheim religion has helped to shape the human intellect; it has been the basis for the earliest civilizations from which the most advanced societies have evolved. It follows, therefore, according to Durkheim, that if we study the most simple society which has ever existed we can reach a greater understanding of the most complex societies. He claims that the simplest and oldest form of religion is that of *totemism*, which is practised by the aborigines of Australia. Aboriginal tribes are divided into clans each having a totem as a symbol which represents it – such as an emu or a kangaroo. These totems are considered to be sacred, and clans hold regular ceremonies at the centre of which is the totem. For Durkheim totemism is the expression, through religion, of the clan's respect and devotion for their community, for when they worship the totem they are in fact worshipping their society. Religious rituals bring the members together at regular intervals and serve to reinforce the social solidarity of the clan.

For Durkheim it is not important to prove whether a system of beliefs is false or wrong; what is important is whether it is true or false for those involved and fulfils a social need. He, therefore, accepts the validity of these views of the world presented by religion as they have a purpose for those who believe in them. Religion also helps to shape and form the content of human knowledge for, by dividing the world up in various ways, such as sacred and non-sacred, it serves to help us make sense of the world around us.

Durkheim and his disciple, Marcel Granet, have used a great deal of anthropological material to illustrate the social origins and functions of knowledge in society. They have, for example, shown the social origins of the categories of understanding such as 'time' and 'space'. These concepts and the ways the different societies understand them are very important, for they influence the way the members of a society see their world.

TIME IN THE WEST

When we think of time in Western society it is difficult not to think of it in terms of a succession of years, months, days and so on. This is not, however, an individual experience as such, but is thought of in a similar way by most people in our society. It is based on a collective system of ideas and measurements to which everyone must conform if society is to run smoothly. In the West, many aspects of life are judged on the basis of this idea of time – the standard of bus services, rates of pay and so forth. Victory and defeat in sport, for example, are often judged with a stop watch. We have come to accept this as the normal, if not natural, way of thinking of time. It is described as a *linear* conception of time and is seen to be extending in a straight line from the past to the future which meet only for a fleeting moment in the present. Linear time is only one among many forms of social time which have existed. It arose as a result of a complex process in which Christianity broke with the pagan view of time which was *cyclical* – that is, that there is no beginning or end – and took from the Old Testament the notion that time does have a beginning and an end, the creation of the world to the coming of the Messiah. In between these events, however, historical time is divided into two main epochs: before and after Christ. The coming of Christ is seen as paving the way for the Messiah and the last judgement.

TIME IN THE EAST

Marcel Granet has shown how the Chinese conception of time is *cyclical*. Just as the seasons reveal the year to be one of a cycle of events, so the division of historical periods is seen to be cyclical. The year is, in fact, only part of a larger cycle of events usually measured in terms of the reigns of emperors and dynasties.

Granet shows how the emperor was seen to be at the centre of Chinese society and his reign was marked by particular temporal and spatial reference points. The beginning of every reign was marked by the establishment of a new centre for the empire.

According to ancient custom the new emperor used to tour his realm to ensure that the various regions were in harmony with the emperor's new calendar. According to Granet, the Chinese conception of time reflected the 'development of a social organization oriented towards an ideal of hierarchy and relative stability'. It was a feudal society which recognized changes in dynasties and emperors but not changes in the existing social order. With the end of a dynasty comes the end of a cycle and the beginning of a new one in the establishment of a new dynasty.

THE CATEGORY OF 'SPACE'

Not only is the conception of time socially conditioned but so also is that of space. According to Durkheim there is no single, pure conception of space for it varies from culture to culture. He

Figure 2.1 **Space: conceptions of space among the aborigines and North American Indians**

There are societies in Australia and North America where space is conceived in the form of an immense circle, because the camp has a circular form; and this spatial circle is divided up exactly like the tribal circle, and is in its image. There are as many regions distinguished as there are clans in the tribe and it is the place occupied by the clans inside the encampments which has determined the orientation of these regions. Each region is defined by the totem of the clan to which it is assigned. Among the Zuni, for example, the pueblo (village) contains seven quarters; each of these is a group of clans which has had a unity: in all probability it was originally a single clan which was later divided. . . .

In the course of history the number of fundamental clans has varied; the number of fundamental regions of space has varied with them. Thus the social organisation has been the model for the spatial organisation and a reproduction of it. It is thus even up to the distinction between right and left which, far from being inherent in the nature of man in general, is very probably the product of representations which are religious and therefore collective.

(E. Durkheim, *The Elementary Forms of Religious Life*, London, George Allen and Unwin, 1975)

illustrates this point with anthropological material on North American Indians and Australian aborigines (see Figure 2.1).

As we can see from Figure 2.1 it is because members of society classify themselves in groups that they are able to think of the physical world in such a way. Again, Durkheim claims that the most simple forms of classification hold the key to the more complex, and it is in totemism that we find the earliest attempts by human beings to order the world in which they live into some sort of coherent unity or what is sometimes called a *cosmology*. The aborigines do this by classifying everything in the natural world in relation to the various clans into which aboriginal society is divided.

Each clan is associated with a particular sacred object, and Durkheim points out that at this stage of development there is not necessarily any logic to such classification, in fact it almost seems arbitrary. There are also strict rules governing each clan's use of things in the natural world, for they are only allowed to eat or use those things associated with the clan.

It can be seen from these examples that the way in which people think is very much influenced by the way society is structured. It is through 'primitive' religion that the logical ordering and understanding of the world by these societies are put into practice and reinforced, and, as we have seen, Durkheim asserts that more advanced modes of thinking such as philosophy and science spring from these simple religions. But in more complex societies religion plays a less central role and the categories of thought which at first had religious connotations have now lost their ceremonial qualities.

The limitations of Durkheim's theory

There are a number of problems with Durkheim's explanation of the relationship between society and religion and the origin of the categories of human understanding. Firstly, much of his anthropological data have been shown to be mistaken and new findings serve to disprove Durkheim's theory. Secondly, there seems to be little connection between science or philosophy and religion. In fact, science and religion are based on different criteria, and, although science does involve faith, ultimately it is judged on the basis of evidence and facts, whereas religion is not.

Finally, Durkheim's stress on society as an organism which

emphasizes unity and a natural movement towards social solidarity does not take account of the fact that there tend to be competing views of reality in any society. Despite the dominance of a particular view of the world there are social groups or classes which often present very different views. This certainly does not seem to be evident in Durkheim's work.

Modern functionalism

Nevertheless, the themes of social unity and cohesion as a natural state of affairs in society was continued by **Talcott Parsons**, who claimed that in order for society to function smoothly it must fulfil four *functional prerequisites*. These are:

1 *goal attainment* – the setting of standards and goals for society to follow;

2 *adaptation* – the necessity to adapt to the environment and to provide the basic needs of society such as food and shelter;

3 *integration* – the maintenance of social order; and

4 *latency* – the creation of the conditions necessary for each individual to perform his or her tasks efficiently and to the best of his ability.

These general functional prerequisites are met by social institutions, each having a number of roles which are guided by a set of fundamental values. For example, the family helps to pass on the norms and values of society through the process of socialization. The child learns from the parents basic principles of behaviour and actions.

Parsons has been criticized, however, for presenting a picture of individuals as being mere products of society or, as Dennis Wrong ('The Oversocialized Conception of Man in Modern Society', 1964) puts it, of developing an 'oversocialized conception of man'. By this he means that Parsons describes a society in which individuals are passively created by being fed with culture. There seems to be little scope for the child to contribute to this process. Phenomenologists would argue that individuals are involved in a two-way process, for not only do they learn from others but they also actively interpret and contribute to the social world around them.

Marxism and the origins of knowledge

As we have seen, Marx recognized that there is a close relationship between ideas and social structure, but he claimed that it was one in which ideas and human consciousness are the products of our material existence. Marx never wrote specifically on the sociology of knowledge but, nevertheless, one of his main concerns was to discover the relationship between knowledge and society. His work in this area is part of a more general social and economic theory called *historical materialism*, which he believed to be the new science of history which could provide answers to human problems that other types of knowledge such as religion and philosophy were unable to provide. By describing historical materialism as a science Marx did not mean this in the conventional sense as it is used by the positivists. It is based on the materialist conception of history in which social, cultural (including knowledge) and political phenomena are determined by the mode of production of material goods in society.

The theory can be summarized by the base–superstructure distinction. The economic base of society – the method of reproducing material existence – influences all other spheres of human existence, which Marx called the superstructure of society and includes the system of ideas. Together they form a particular mode of production such as feudalism or capitalism. Each mode of production produces a set of ideas or an ideology which serves to support the position of those who hold power.

Capitalism

Marx concentrated mainly on the capitalist mode of production, and he showed how during the Industrial Revolution Britain and other European countries were transformed into urban societies dominated by a system of factory production which subjected large numbers of people to the dehumanizing effects of early factory conditions. He showed how during this period there emerged a ruling class ideology which serves to justify the position of the capitalists (bourgeoisie).

These ideas help to hide from the proletariat the exploitative nature of capitalism. In fact, Marx sees the interests of the proletariat and the bourgeoisie as diametrically opposed. The proletariat own nothing but their labour power which they sell to the bourgeoisie, who seek to maximize their profits by paying the proletariat as little as possible. However, the ideas of the bourgeoisie prevail and the system is seen to be fair. Because they have been taken in by bourgeois ideology, Marx asserted that the working class suffers from a 'false consciousness' – that is, they are unable to see the truth lurking behind bourgeois ideology.

Ideology and truth

If ideologies only present a partial picture of reality then how do we gain a true picture of society? Marx claimed that historical materialism is the only non-ideological knowledge which exists, and the only group of people who can acquire this knowledge is the working class. Before this can occur, however, the working class must become a united force which is aware of the contradictions of capitalism and realizes its historic mission to establish a communist society. In Marx's words, it must become a 'class for itself'.

The proletariat is the only class which can do this because it has no vested interest in capitalism and has 'nothing to lose but its chains'. Under communism, all property will be communally owned, and this will mean that there will be no capitalist property owners to exploit the workers. This will lead to a classless society with no ruling class ideology, for the egalitarian ideas of the proletariat will prevail.

The limitations of Marx's theory

Marx's theory of the origin and effect of ideas in society is criticized by some sociologists for being too simplistic, especially in terms of his explanation of the relationship between the economic base and the superstructure of society. He claims that within each mode of production there arises a set of ideas, but he does not show how ruling class ideology comes to prevail, nor the way in which it is transmitted by the various institutions of the superstructure, such as the education system or the mass media.

Because Marx's theory of the relationship between the economic base and superstructure is not fully worked out it has been open to various interpretations. One extreme interpretation of Marx's theory is that of the *vulgar Marxists* who see a straightforward relationship between the economic base and the superstructure. They claim that the way a society is organized depends to a large extent upon the economic relations of production. Thus, within the capitalist mode of production, for example, there will automatically emerge a set of legal, political and educational institutions which will transmit capitalist ruling class ideology. A theory which explains all social phenomena in terms of the economic structure is known as *economic determinism*. Many sociologists would argue that the relationship between the economic base and the superstructure is much more complex. Marx himself was not a determinist, and even suggested that the superstructure will interact with, and even influence, the economic base.

Modern Marxism and the theory of knowledge

A primary concern of modern Marxists has been to develop further Marx's theory of the relationship between the economic base and the superstructure of society, especially in the light of the changes which have occurred in the capitalist system since Marx's death, and also to break away from determinist explanations of this relationship. One important aspect of modern capitalism is that it has proved to be more resilient than Marx had expected, for there has been no revolution in Western Europe which has managed to overthrow capitalism. Marxists such as Antonio Gramsci and Louis Althusser became interested in the role of ideology in the survivial of capitalism.

Ideology and modern capitalism

Gramsci was one of the first to break with the traditional division of society by Marxists into the economic base and superstructure in which the former was seen to be of primary importance. Instead, Gramsci stresses the importance of culture and ideology, both for the domination of society by the bourgeoisie and also for a potentially revolutionary working class. He claims that once the bourgeoisie has gained ideological dominance over society its power rests not primarily on its ownership and control of the means of production but on its cultural and ideological hegemony.

'Hegemony' is a broad term which is used by Gramsci to

denote bourgeois domination in its widest sense, not only in the field of politics and intellectual life, but also in the realm of 'commonsense'. It is based on the voluntary acceptance of the ideas of the dominant class and becomes even more effective if this class is able to incorporate its ideas into the commonsense view of the world possessed by the working class. This usually involves the notion that there is such a thing as a natural order to the world – the implications of this being that if the subordinate class believes something to be natural then it cannot be changed. Within capitalism the idea that the upper and middle classes have 'breeding' serves as a commonsense explanation that they are born to lead.

Gramsci does not see ideologies in terms of their truth or false-hood, but according to their power to bind together the members of social classes and to put into practice particular views of how society should be organized. He also recognizes the importance of an ideological apparatus which helps to secure the consent of the dominated class. In capitalist society this involves institutions such as the family and the education system which help to spread and maintain the dominance of ruling class ideology.

Structuralism – Althusser

The structuralist Marxist **Althusser** is also concerned with the relationship between the economic base and the superstructure, because he too objects to the deterministic interpretations of Marx's theory. He claims that the various elements of the super-structure are independent or, in Althusser's words, 'relatively autonomous' of the economic base which is dominant 'only in the last instance'. However, unlike Gramsci, who actually explains the process of ideological domination and how it is experienced by the working class, Althusser concentrates purely on the insti-tutional nature of this ideological domination.

For Althusser, every mode of production is a complex inter-action between the economy, ideology and politics. The ideo-logical and political aspects of the social formation are part of the superstructure and play a vital role in helping to reproduce the existing mode of production. In an attempt to explain this role he develops the concepts of *ideological state apparatuses* (ISAs) and *repressive state apparatuses* (RSAs). The RSAs include the various branches of the state such as the police, the army and the judiciary which use force that is regarded as legitimate to deal with threats to the capitalist system. However, the RSAs are only used when the ISAs have failed. It is through the ISAs, which include institutions such as the educational system, the family, religion and the media, that the state can communicate ideologies and thus help to reproduce the capitalist system.

Problems with modern Marxism

One problem which modern Marxists have tried to tackle is how to bring about the overthrow of capitalism. Marx claimed that this could only happen when the working class develops a revolutionary class consciousness – that is, consciousness to further their interests in opposition to the bourgeoisie – and decides to overthrow the existing exploitative system. It was left to later Marxists to figure out how this could be achieved.

According to Gramsci, this can be done by raising the consciousness and cultural level of the proletariat – 'by educating them and making them aware of the posibility of an alternative society'. To this end he was involved in the Workers' Council Movement in the industrial areas of Italy in the inter-war years. From Gramsci's theory, therefore, we have the basis of a strategy whereby men and women can change the circumstances of their existence. Althusser's theory, however, provides no such strategy, for by concentrating almost exclusively on the structures of the capitalist system he offers no explanation of how to raise the consciousness of the working class.

Some Marxists have become disillusioned with the proletariat as a revolutionary class. The members of the Frankfurt School (Marcuse, Horkheimer, Adorno), for example, claim that because of the relative material affluence enjoyed by the working class, in modern capitalism they are completely blinded by a false consciousness which makes them believe in capitalism. Herbert Marcuse claims that only those groups in society which have no interest in the system have the potential to develop a revolutionary consciousness, and he identifies students and oppressed racial minorities as the possible leaders of a new revolutionary force.

Despite these attempts to develop and modify Marx's theory in the light of the changes in modern capitalism, Marxists have had little success in their aims to overthrow capitalism. What they have done, however, is to identify the important role played by ideology and ideas in general in helping to support the capitalist system.

Karl Mannheim

Karl Mannheim was one of the first sociologists to write specifically on the sociology of knowledge and also one of the first sociologists directly to confront the problem of relativism. In Mannheim's sociology of knowledge all ideas and knowledge are seen to be determined by history and are, therefore, changeable.

It was Marx who claimed that ideas and knowledge are the products of people's material condition and that every mode of production produces a set of ideas and beliefs – an ideology – which help to support the existing social structure. For Marx, however, not all ideas are ideological, but for Mannheim they are. With the exception of natural science and mathematics, he claims that all ideas and beliefs are determined by the social existence of those who hold them. Because groups in society differ in their views of the world, there is no absolute standard whereby we can judge what is true and what is false. However, he did distinguish between two types of knowledge: 'ideological' and 'utopian'. Neither of these types of knowledge explains the world as it is; and for this reason he calls them 'situationally transcendent' – that is, they go beyond reality. The difference between them, however, is that *ideologies* tend to support the existing social order and the interests of certain groups, while *utopias* are ideas held by groups who tend to disagree with the existing social order and propose an alternative system. Mannheim recognized that in every historical period there have been ideas which point to alternative social systems, but he claims that these were not utopian because they did not advocate revolutionary change within the existing society. In the feudal period, for example, the expectation of future prosperity and equality of all citizens was confined to the future kingdom of God, not on earth. As such, those ideas functioned pretty much as part of the existing feudal ideology which supported the status quo. Ideologies only become utopian when certain groups try to put into practice their vision of a future society. The communist–socialist utopia is one such example.

The role of the sociology of knowledge, for Mannheim, is to

explain the connection between the social existence of people in a particular socio-historical context and the world view which they possess – be it ideological or utopian. The way the sociologist is to do this, according to Mannheim, is by using the phenomenological method of placing oneself in the position of the people being studied. In this way, the sociologist can better understand that particular group's world view. He calls this the 'documentary method of interpretation', which starts from the assumption that there is no meaning in society other than that which actors (people) themselves place upon the social interactions they engage in. Each society or group within society will, therefore, see the world differently, and there is, for Mannheim, no objective standard whereby we can judge the truth of a particular view of the world.

Relationism – a solution to the problem of relativism?

Mannheim's theory has been criticized for not providing any standard whereby we can judge ideas and beliefs. In an attempt to avoid such criticisms he gives special status to social scientific knowledge which is produced by the 'free-floating intelligentsia'. In his later work Mannheim argued that a relatively classless intelligentsia created the right conditions for the production of knowledge which has a greater truth content than any other knowledge. This 'socially unattached' group has access to such knowledge because it is less affected by ideological motives and can, therefore, look beyond class-based knowledge. The knowledge this group produced was seen by Mannheim to have practical application, for he believed that it could be used to reconcile and synthesize the views of extreme groups holding ideological or utopian ideas. This would result in a 'total world view' in which all aspects such as feminism, communism, socialism and conservatism would be included. Mannheim calls this new theoretical position 'relationism', which he thinks is able to overcome the problems of relativism, for although he still believes that absolute truth cannot be achieved, it is possible to get closer to it by the relational sociology of knowledge. To what extent such a synthesis can be achieved is questionable.

Mannheim's relationist theory is seen by some sociologists to be just another form of relativism. This is because he does not consider the fact that the social background and education of the free-floating intelligentsia may cause them to hold views which are no less ideological than any other group. Indeed, intellectuals on the whole tend to be a priviledged group who benefit more than most from the system in which they live. Their command of vast amounts of knowledge is no guarantee that they have special access to the truth. In an attempt to test Mannheim's theory K. Danziger ('Ideology and Utopia in South Africa', 1973) carried out a study of the intelligentsia of South Africa. He found no evidence to show that they were producing a synthesis of all the competing views in that country, such as those of the conservative Afrikaners and the black nationalists, in the desire to provide a solution to the problem of apartheid.

In his sociology of knowledge Mannheim tries to combine aspects of both Marxism and phenomenology to create his own solution to the problem of relativism, and, as we will see in following chapters, more recent developments in this field are also the result of a combination of theories. A further feature of recent developments in the sociology of knowledge is that there has been a shift away from general sociological theories of the origins of knowledge towards more detailed studies of the specific sources of knowledge in society such as education, science and religion, which will now be examined.

3 The sources of knowledge in society – science

Introduction

Throughout our lives we encounter a wide variety of sources of knowledge. Religion, as we have seen, has long acted as an institution which has provided us with a view of the world and our place in the universe. The state is another institution which is an important generator of knowledge. It regularly produces documents and publishes statistics which are used as the basis for official policy and are supposed to keep us informed about all aspects of society from the size of the population to the rate of unemployment. Scientific institutions such as universities and research institutes are also involved in the process of imparting knowledge to the population. Scientific breakthroughs and discoveries are continually being made, and scientists are held in particularly high esteem for the knowledge they produce because of their ability to solve many of our practical problems. Recognizing the importance of these institutions as sources of knowledge, sociologists have begun to shift their research away from general explanations of the nature of knowledge in society and to concentrate on specific areas. Recently, for example, the education system and the knowledge taught in school has come under close scrutiny, and sociologists involved in research in this area have begun to question many of our basic assumptions about what we are taught at school.

Science

Natural scientific knowledge such as chemistry and physics have long been given special status by sociologists. Durkheim and Mannheim, for example, regarded it as a pure form of knowledge relatively untouched by social factors. Indeed, science is still seen by many to be the most objective and value-free form of knowledge that has ever existed and the products of science are plain for all to see. From the earliest feats of engineering such as the Pyramids, to the landing of men on the moon, science has projected human-kind from the stone age to the space age.

To a great extent our image of natural scientific knowledge is influenced by the notion of scientists as neutral observers of nature who, by using the scientific method, have the potential to solve the world's problems.

The scientific method

The scientific method can be seen as part of an unwritten set of rules and procedures one could call the 'scientific code of conduct'. It is thought to be the best way of producing objective scientific knowledge, and involves the following principles:

1 *observation* – the scientist systematically observes and records what he or she sees;
2 *hypothesis formation* – the scientist comes up with a *hypothesis* or proposition concerning what has been observed and tests it by experimentation;
3 *experimentation* – this will help to prove or disprove the hypothesis;
4 *scientific laws* – on the basis of experimental results scientists will be able to develop general explanations or laws which help to explain certain phenomena (for example, Newton's hypothesis about the existence of gravity and its effects has been confirmed many times by experiment and has come to be known as 'the law of gravity');
5 *theory formation* – this involves ordering all the laws into a theory or a model which will enable the scientist to explain wide-ranging problems such as the origin and nature of the universe;
6 *flexibility* – scientists should be prepared to change, modify or reject their theories in the light of new evidence;
7 results should be open to scrutiny: all scientists should present their findings for scrutiny to other experts in the field, which enables others to check and even replicate their work; and
8 *objectivity* – scientists should be objective observers of the natural world and their research must be motivated only by the desire to increase scientific knowledge.

This code of conduct is believed to be based on logical principles and has a built-in mechanism to ensure that the work of unscrupulous scientists is easily detected. It is also thought to be the best way of enabling scientists to uncover the secrets of the universe and ultimately to discover the 'truth'.

The hypothetico-deductive model

Philosophers of science, however, have come to question the notion that scientists, following the scientific method, can discover the truth. Instead they have come up with a more modest theory of what science can do which is based on the *hypothetico-deductive model*. It is in the work of **Karl Popper** that this model finds its most comprehensive explanation. In his book entitled *The Logic of Scientific Discovery* (1934) Popper claims that there is no such thing as 'objective truth' in science. He argues that it is a myth that scientists practise their craft by pure observation because they all start with a particular view of the world which inevitably affects their results. The truth may exist but we will never find it.

All we can hope for is a partial understanding of the physical world. Because of this Popper claims that all scientific knowledge is provisional and open to rejection or refutation by new discoveries. In his book *Conjectures and Refutations* (1963) Popper outlines in detail this method of scientific inquiry. He claims that the most rational procedure for any scientist is to develop a hypothesis or conjecture which serves to explain a particular phenomenon and then to do his or her best to refute it. Those hypotheses which, after rigorous testing, have been proved false are rejected, and those which have not been falsified are accepted as making a contribution to scientific knowledge. However, we can never claim to have discovered the truth even if a hypothesis has been tested a million times without being falsified. For example, we may hypothesize that all swans are white and from our observations this might seem to be the case. However, the hypothesis cannot be said to be *true* because there is always the possibility that black swans exist, as indeed they do.

Origins of the sociology of science

The earliest studies in the sociology of science did not tend to get involved in debates about the nature of scientific knowledge, but tended to concentrate on the role of science in society. The work of the American sociologist **R. K. Merton** is perhaps the best-known of the pioneering studies in this field. Being a functionalist Merton sees society as a system which is divided into a number of subsystems each in its own way contributing to the stability of society, the institution of science being one of those sub-systems. Merton was much concerned with explaining the most favourable conditions for scientific progress to take place and thus make the most effective contribution to the smooth running of society. This involved an analysis of the wider society in which science operates as well as of the norms and values governing the institution of science.

The ethos of science

Broadly speaking, Merton identifies four aspects of the scientific ethos, which he refers to as *institutional imperatives*. These institutional imperatives or norms act together to promote the goal of extending 'certified knowledge' and thus benefiting society. The institutional imperatives are listed below.

1 *Universalism*: This requires the scientific community to judge and evaluate all scientific discoveries and research purely on the basis of objective criteria. A person's race or creed should play no part in this for they have no bearing on the truth content of a scientific claim. For example, an anti-semite cannot declare Einstein's theory of relativity to be invalid just because Einstein was a Jew.

2 *Communism*: By this Merton refers to the public ownership of scientific knowledge. Progress in science occurs precisely because it is a communal enterprise and scientists share their knowledge. Without such co-operation the progress of science would be severely affected. The only rights a scientist has to the knowledge which he or she has contributed to the community are those of recognition and esteem.

3 *Disinterestedness*: According to Merton, one of the great merits of scientists is that they are motivated by the desire to gain knowledge purely for its own sake. He argues that this does not occur because scientists are innately more honest than the rest of us but because of the institutional controls exerted over

them. He claims that the relative absence of fraud in science compared to other disciplines is the result of the strict policing within the scientific community.

4 *Organized scepticism*: The success of science, for Merton, is to a great extent due to its detached nature. It looks at the world objectively, unaffected by tradition or superstition.

In his book entitled *The Scientific Community* (1965) **W. O. Hagstrom** investigates further the institutional factors which help to minimize the incidence of deviant behaviour such as fraud in science. Hagstrom points to the need among scientists to receive the recognition of their peers. For this to occur, however, a scientist must make regular offerings of 'gifts' to the scientific community which take the form of publishable material. In this way scientific claims can be scrutinized by other scientists. The reward for this comes in the form of recognition through the publication of articles in learned journals or, in cases of particular merit, election to prestigious societies or the award of a Nobel Prize. The training period which scientists undergo is seen by Hagstrom to be an important period of socialization which helps to promote uniformity between them. Should this training period fail to stop a scientist from adopting a deviant means of gaining recognition, the exchange system will no doubt expose any fraud.

THE MYTH OF THE SCIENTIFIC ETHOS
Studies of science in the Mertonian tradition take it for granted that science develops according to the principles outlined above. Recent studies, however, show that at certain times these norms have not guided the work of scientists (see Figure 3.1).

The sociologist **M. Mulkay** uses the Velikovsky affair to show that at certain times the ethos of science plays no part in the work of scientists. Having adhered to the ethos of science by presenting his data to other scientists for scrutiny he was met with rejection. When in 1946 he approached Professor Harlow Shapley with a request for help, Shapley refused, pointing out that Velikovsky's theory was inconsistent with the theory of gravitation, and Shapley even refused to read Velikovsky's book. Had the institutional imperatives described by Merton been effective, Velikovsky's work would have been greeted by an open-minded scientific community which would be prepared to give it detailed and objective examination. Instead, it was quite evident that

Figure 3.1 **The Velikovsky affair**
In 1950 Immanuel Velikovsky published a book in the USA
which was to put the scientific ethos to the test in an
extreme way. The book, entitled *Worlds in Collision* made
a number of remarkable claims which posed a challenge to
the entire spectrum of established science from astronomy
to zoology. Briefly stated, Velikovsky's book tries to show
that the present state of the world and its inhabitants is not
the result of some languorous and almost imperceptible
process of evolution, but rather due to a number of violent
and cataclysmic events which shook the earth. Velikovsky
claimed that the universe is not the harmonious place that
astronomers seem to believe but is in fact unstable and
subject to regular periods of upheaval. He points to the Bible
which contains descriptions of many unexplained natural
disasters, most of which are thought to be apocryphal, to
back up his claims.

Much of what Velikovsky claimed was speculative but he
presented his data for scrutiny to other scientists and now
all that remained was for the scientific community to receive
his theory in the spirit of organized scepticism and disinterestedness. Instead it was rejected by almost all the scientists
Velikovsky approached:

> Throughout the story of Velikovsky's reception by
> science, one phenomenon occurs over and over again.
> One prominent scientist after another undertakes to crit-
> icize and ridicule the author and his theories; having done
> this he states – not without a trace of pride – that he has not
> read the books.
> (R. E. Jurgens in *The Velikovsky Affair*, A. De Grazia
> (ed.), London, Abacus, 1978).

Velikovsky's scientific colleagues had violated the norms of
universalism, communism and organized scepticism. Mulkay
argues that this example shows the unwillingness of scientists to
be open minded about new ways of seeing the world and their
general inability to think outside what **T. Kuhn** calls accepted
'paradigms' (see Figure 3.2).

Figure 3.2 **Scientific paradigms**
A paradigm refers to the accepted procedures and ways of thinking within a particular discipline. The laws of mechanics constitute a paradigm and scientists are aware of what should or should not happen in terms of the paradigm. Velikovsky's claim that the universe is an unstable place was at odds with the laws of mechanics therefore it was rejected just as in the past new theories which contradicted the established paradigm were rejected, for example, Darwin's theory of evolution. An established paradigm is not necessarily the only or best way of looking at the world, but it happens to be the one which the established scientific community adheres to. Darwin, for example, had very sound scientific arguments to back up his case and there were also other scientists who supported his views.

The new sociology of science

Broad and Wade (*Betrayers of the Truth*, 1982) describe the ethos of science as the 'prevailing ideology' of science, for like any ideology, it contains some truth but is an imperfect description of how science works. Recently, sociologists have taken the bold step of investigating how scientists go about their work and of critically analysing the theoretical assumptions and the methods they adopt in their research.

Events such as the Velikovsky affair and the work of Mulkay led a number of sociologists to claim that not only is knowledge in general a social product but so also is scientific knowledge. Two sociologists who represent what has come to be known as the 'Edinburgh School', **B. Barnes** and **D. Bloor**, argue that scientific knowledge should not be looked at differently from other forms of accepted knowledge. They further claim that what is important in studying science is not whether the knowledge produced by scientists is true or not, but the reasons why scientists pursue particular research programmes and why they adhere to certain beliefs and not others. In his book entitled *Knowledge* *and Social Imagery* (1976), Bloor claims that truth and objectivity are social constructs produced by scientists in the process of creating scientific knowledge. In his book *Scientific Knowledge and Sociological Theory* (1974), Barnes points to the factors involved in the production of scientific knowledge, which are often economic, social, political and even religious. Take the example of ballistics (the study of projectile trajectories) which experienced rapid development during the seventeenth century. This was certainly not a subject adopted by natural philosophers out of pure scientific interest but was very much a product of the age – that is, the development of the art of warfare using firearms. Thus, for Bloor and Barnes scientific knowledge very much depends upon the interests and social environment of the scientists who produce it. This view, as we will see later, is similar to recent Marxist interpretations of the nature of science in society.

Phenomenology and the sociology of science

Recently, developments have taken a more phenomenological turn, in which scientific knowledge is seen as a product of the social interaction between scientists and between scientists and their equipment. Adopting the method developed by Berger and Luckmann in *The Social Construction of Reality*, the 'Constructivist School', as it is called, argues that scientists do not describe scientific reality as it might exist but they are actively engaged in a process of constructing scientific reality.

K. Knorr-Cetina points out in her article 'Towards a Constructivist Interpretation of Science' (1983) that a laboratory is a disorganized place, and when scientists get together in such an environment and try to make sense of and select from the huge mass of data which it is possible to collect, the end product is the result of a process of negotiation between scientists. Selection, however, according to Knorr-Cetina, is highly influenced by what the scientists as a group believe and what they think their superiors or grant-giving bodies would like to hear. She concludes by saying that scientists are not guided in their work by the universal principles of the scientific method but produce knowledge which is very much dependent on the context and environment in which the scientists are working.

The language of science

Recent research has also focused on the language used by scientists in the process of constructing scientific knowledge. Gilbert and Mulkay in their article entitled 'Contexts of Scientific Discourse' (1980) show how scientists use two different types of language: one for their published accounts; and another in the more informal discussions with their research colleagues. After conducting a number of interviews and examining the research reports of a group of scientists, Gilbert and Mulkay argue that published reports are not written to give a genuine, objective explanation of research findings but are in fact subtle devices designed to convince the reader of the validity of the scientist's results. They found that scientists are very selective about what they publish and what they report is dependent on a number of factors such as beliefs and views of the group involved in a research project. For example, a group of scientists involved in a research programme will be unlikely to publish facts and figures which could be used by a group proposing an alternative theory.

According to Gilbert and Mulkay, what is important in research reports is what tends to be left out, for scientists are concerned with presenting their findings and theories in such a way as to make them convincing. Thus, the niggling doubts and uncertainties of the researchers are left out and as a result the formal presentation of a researcher's findings 'begin to take on an appearance of objectivity' (Gilbert and Mulkay, 1980). This objectivity is strengthened by the fact that authors of research reports are required to write a separate section on the methods used in an experiment. This account must be of sufficient detail to enable any competent scientist to reproduce the experiment. However, of the researchers interviewed by Gilbert and Mulkay it was a common admission that exact replication of the results of another scientist's experiment are 'virtually impossible'. Indeed, many of the scientists interviewed informally did not expect to be able to replicate an experiment from a Methods Section of a report. Many of the scientists in fact stressed that it was almost impossible to describe adequately in words experimental skills which can only be learned by observation and experience.

The work of Gilbert and Mulkay is highly revealing in terms of the way in which scientists actively construct scientific knowledge and do not tend to adhere to the norms of the scientific ethos, although this might appear to be the case in their published findings. Furthermore, self-policing of the scientific community is made that much more difficult because of the problem of replication.

How does scientific progress occur?

If it is the case that science does not operate in the way the ethos of science dictates and the scientific community tends to be rather conservative and reluctant to see the world outside its own tried and tested theoretical perspectives, how does scientific progress occur?

Thomas Kuhn and the structure of scientific revolutions

One of the philosophers to question the traditional view of how science operates is **Thomas Kuhn** in his book *The Structure of Scientific Revolutions* (1962). Here Kuhn claims that, contrary to popular belief, scientific communities are not noted for their open-mindedness but for their conservatism, which is a result of the socialization of scientists within a particular intellectual tradition. They are, in other words, taught to think in terms of a particular *paradigm* which, as we have seen, is a school of thought on how scientists should approach their subject and what to look for while conducting their research (see Figure 3.3).

Once a paradigm is accepted by a scientific community, according to Kuhn there begins a period of 'normal science' in which scientists are engaged in a kind of 'mopping up' operation. Their research is mainly concerned with filling in the gaps and solving the problems posed by the paradigm. When anomalies arise it is usually the researcher's theory or his or her experimental technique which is blamed rather than the paradigm. Nevertheless, according to Kuhn, there comes a time when these anomalies become so pervasive that they cannot be ignored and scientists are forced to raise questions about accepted beliefs. This tends to result in a period of intellectual and social upheaval often involving bitter exchanges between the representatives of competing theories. A classic example of this was the meeting of the British Association for the Advancement of Science which took place at Oxford in 1860 during which the Creationists, led

Figure 3.3 **Paradigmatic science – the story of light**
A good example of how a paradigm works is the way in which scientists have tried to understand the phenomenon of light. During the late nineteenth century physicists believed that light was an electromagnetic force but nobody could explain how it got from one place to another. Scientists busied themselves with trying to solve this problem but it was generally accepted that light had to pass through some sort of medium or substance which would support it. They called this substance the 'luminiferous aether' and spent the next half-century trying to prove its existence. The aether was supposed to fill all space and was thought to possess the apparently contradictory qualities of being permeable but at the same time rigid and thus able to support the light passing though it. So went the paradigm. But despite their belief in the aether scientists have not been able to detect it.

by William Wilberforce, launched an attack on Darwin's theory of evolution. This meeting marked a period of open conflict between the greatest minds of the scientific community and resulted in the slow but sure adoption of Darwin's new and revolutionary ideas. There had in fact been a *scientific revolution* in which one scientific paradigm replaced another. Scientists began to change their allegiance from Creationism to the theory of evolutionary change.

In comparing this to a religious conversion, Kuhn is emphasizing the fact that there is no logical reason why the new paradigm should be accepted, for it cannot be tested using the old methods, and, to begin with, it raises more questions than it answers. Above all, the new paradigm ensures that the world, or aspects of it, will never be seen in the same way again. For example, when Copernicus's model of the universe was accepted the earth was no longer seen as the stationary body at the centre of the universe but as one of many planets revolving around the sun. From Kuhn's theory it would seem that science on the whole does not develop by steady progression, each new development logically following previous ones, leading to some kind of universal truth. The history of science can instead be seen more as a series of discontinuous phases marked by periods of intense struggle between competing paradigms which have few or no common points of reference.

Paul Feyerabend and the 'irrationalist' view of science

In his book *Against Method* (1975), **Feyerabend** makes the intriguing claim that science is in fact an irrational enterprise, for at no time in history has there been an objective scientific method. He goes on to argue that the only time scientific progress has been made is when scientists have dared to break with the existing conventions rather than when they adhere to them. Feyerabend suggests that the only way forward in science is to follow the example of those scientists in the past who have flouted convention and adopted the philosophy of 'anything goes'. He sees the scientific community today as acting very much as the Church did in medieval times by stifling creativity and branding nonconformists as heretics.

Marxism and science

Marxists have tended to look at science not as an irrational enterprise, nor as a body of knowledge produced by a community of scientists guided by the ethos of science but rather as a body of knowledge and practical skills which have developed as a result of demands of the economic system. They have criticized conventional Western sociology of science, which they claim concentrates on the work of individual scientists engaged in the disinterested pursuit of knowledge. The result has been to view science as a relatively independent subsystem with a self-governing community.

It is in the work of the Soviet physicist **Boris Hessen** that we find one of the first systematic attempts to develop a Marxist theory of science. In 1931 Hessen made a speech to the International Congress of the History of Science and Technology in London in which he claimed that modern science has developed directly as a result of the needs of capitalism. For Hessen then, science must be analysed in terms of its wider social and economic context, because this will show that the driving force of science is not the objective pursuit of knowledge but the profit motive. Scientific knowledge has been harnessed, in both its pure and applied form, for the process of commodity production, such as factories and so on.

In his book *The Social Functions of Science* (1939), **J. D. Bernal** develops the ideas of Hessen by showing how science has been used to generate profit and is also used by the state in the maintenance of its power. However, this relationship between capitalism and science is based on a fundamental contradiction, according to J. D. Bernal, because the potential that science has for the elimination of human suffering, such as disease and poverty, is continually frustrated by the emphasis which capitalism places on profit. Bernal advocated the development of a truly 'socialist science' based on the idea that science should be for the people and that this can only be achieved if we plan for the future needs of society. **S. and H. Rose** (*Ideology in/of the Natural Sciences*, eds., 1979) point out that we only have to look at the Soviet Union to see that planning alone is not enough. They claim that it is not only in the Western capitalist countries but also in Eastern Europe that science has become the tool of the state. In both East and West science is used to maintain the power of the state and to oppress their citizens. This involves everything from anti-riot equipment and weapons to the development of ever more effective nuclear deterrents.

What then would constitute a 'socialist science'? Marxists are as yet unable to answer this question. Marx did write of the potentially liberating effect of science on society but there is little in his work to show how this can be achieved.

4 The sources of knowledge in society – religion

Science and religion as belief systems

It is perhaps no coincidence that sociologists and philosophers have made a comparison between science and religion as belief systems. A belief system is a set of beliefs and ideas which help people to make sense of and interpret the world. It also tends to be supported and promoted by a community of experts who claim to have a special insight into the truth. For example, in religion we have the clergy and in science we have the scientists. Emile Durkheim was in fact one of the first to point to the connection between religion and other forms of knowledge for, as we have seen in Chapter 2, Durkheim claimed that it is through religion that human beings first attempted to interpret the world and it is from religion that more advanced ways of thinking, such as science, evolved. In their book *The Social Construction of Reality*, Berger and Luckmann go so far as to claim that a sociology of knowledge without a sociology of religion is impossible (and vice versa). We have already seen how Berger and Luckmann claim that in all societies there exists a universe of meaning which becomes institutionalized and is seen as *the* true and objective way of seeing the world. They claim that in the past religion has probably been the most important source of legitimation for any universe of meaning, providing important ways of justifying a particular view of the world. Over time, however, there may develop competing universes of meaning, one of which may dominate. In the Middle Ages, for example, religion was the dominant belief system which provided the 'official' version of how the world and the universe should be seen. There was slowly developing, however, an alternative belief system which was to pose a serious challenge to the religious world view, but the threat of the scientific world view is a relatively recent phenomenon.

The social reality of religion

In his book *The Social Reality of Religion* (1973) Peter Berger explains the role played by religion in the past in providing comprehensive structures of meaning in a world of chaos and uncertainty. He claims that it is natural for humans to try and impose order on the world, and this is inevitably a social process because we are social beings who are unable to survive on our own.

The threat to social order

The order imposed upon the world by individuals in society, however, is constantly under threat, according to Berger, which takes the form of unexplained phenomena such as natural disasters and death. This is because they threaten the smooth and ordered functioning of society. In an effort to explain such things and to give them meaning, humans place them within the realm of awesome and mysterious powers and develop a body of knowledge and ideas which Berger calls a '*cosmology*'.

According to Berger, it is the social organization and practice of beliefs in a cosmology which constitute a religion and involve the division of the world into the *sacred* and *profane*. Something which is sacred stands out in society as having strange or potentially dangerous powers which, through special ceremonies, can be harnessed for the good of the community. The sacred include phenomena or objects which have significance outside everyday experience and inspire acts of devotion and worship. For example, during the Middle Ages in England Christians made regular pilgrimages to the shrine of Thomas à Becket at Canterbury in the hope of receiving the blessing of the saint and to make penance. Anything can be made sacred by a society – from a rock or animal to a person, such as a chief. Although the sacred is set apart from the rest of society by ritual, the profane world refers to the secular side of life involving the everyday realities such as work and the satisfaction of basic needs. Within a sacred cosmology unexplained phenomena find an explanation and an individual receives answers to questions of ultimate meaning. It provides a comprehensive framework able to provide definitive answers to all spheres of life from the mundane to the mysterious. The threat to social order is thus reduced.

The problem of definition

Berger's definition of religion involves more than what most sociologists understand by the term. He calls it an 'inclusive' definition, because it encompasses most systems of belief which provide answers to questions of ultimate meaning.

It should be stressed that Berger does make a distinction between religious belief systems and non-religious belief systems. For example, although Marxism is a comprehensive system of beliefs, Berger does not go so far as to call it a religion. Luckmann, on the other hand, does, and in his book *The Invisible Religion* (1967) he argues that any human attempt to comprehend our place in the cosmos is *ipso facto* religious. Nevertheless, having made this distinction we can still say that Berger and Luckmann use an inclusive definition of religion as it includes many more, or in the case of Luckmann, all belief systems not traditionally thought of as religious – for example, scientology and psychologism. These involve using the techniques of modern science and psychology to help individuals cope with the pressures of modern life.

Religion and legitimation – explaining misfortune

One of the most important aspects of a religion, according to Berger, is its ability to explain such phenomena as evil, suffering and death. The explanation of such things in religious terms is known as a '*theodicy*' (see Figure 4.1). Berger takes this term from the work of **Max Weber**; it literally means 'the justice of God'. Weber calls a theodicy any socially accepted explanation for human suffering and injustice, and in classic Western theology it involves reconciling the apparently contradictory beliefs in a benevolent and omnipotent God with the existence of a world full of evil and suffering.

The plausibility of religious belief systems

In order for such a religious view of the world to exist it must have a firm social base. In the words of Berger, it must have a 'plausibility structure' which, in simple terms, refers to the social

Figure 4.1 **The theodicy of Hinduism**

All the major world religions possess a theodicy, according to Weber, who claims that the most comprehensive and rational of these is that of Hinduism which is based on an adherence to the notion of *reincarnation* and the doctrine of *Karma*. Reincarnation is the idea that a person lives a number of lives and Karma is the doctrine that every human act in some way affects a person in their next life as well as the present. As a result, Hinduism preaches that everyone, no matter how unfortunate, deserves to be in the situation they are in. Those at the bottom of the caste system, the 'untouchables', therefore have no cause to complain. By the same token, those that are at the top, e.g. the Brahmins, need not feel any guilt, for they too deserve what they have. It can be seen how a theodicy legitimates the position of the powerful and the powerless. In this way, Berger claims that Weber's theory of religion goes further than Marx's which mainly looks at religion as an 'opiate' for the oppressed. Such beliefs have encouraged acceptance of the existing order through the desire to live a good Hindu life in the hope of reaching the *Atman-Brahman* – a condition of unity between the individual, the universe and the Creator.

system in which the beliefs are located. Destruction of a plausibility structure also implies the collapse of a universe of meaning. As an example of this Berger uses the demise of the Inca religion resulting from the Spanish conquest of Peru.

> Thus, for example, the religious world of pre-Columbian Peru was objectively and subjectively real as long as its plausibility structure, namely pre-Columbian Inca society, remained intact. . . . Conversely, when the conquering Spaniards destroyed this plausibility structure the reality of the world based on it began to disintegrate with terrifying rapidity.
> (P. Berger, *The Social Reality of Religion*, Harmondsworth, Penguin University Books, 1973, p. 54)

This destruction of Inca society led to the redefinition of reality and the establishment of a new universe of meaning under the

Spaniards. But the collapse of a plausibility structure need not take such a violent and conclusive form. The gradual *secularization* of Western society can be seen as the result of a number of challenges to the plausibility structure of Christianity. By 'secularization' Berger means the 'process by which sectors of society and culture are removed from the domination of religious institutions and symbols' (Berger, *The Social Reality of Religion*, p. 113).

Secularization of the West

For Berger, the process of secularization does not mean that religion is declining in importance in Western society, as **Bryan Wilson** (1966) would suggest, but that there is no longer a belief system dominated by a single religious universe of meaning. There are now competing belief systems, some religious, some scientific and some a combination of both.

Secularization presents itself as a process which for Berger has no single cause, for he sees it as the product of the complex interplay between material and ideal factors. One of the most important material 'carriers' of secularization, according to Berger, is industrial capitalism and the revolutionary change which it brought about, such as the upheavals of early urbanization and the exposure to alternative world views through the advances in mass transportation and communication which have acted to undermine the plausibility structure of Christianity.

Perhaps the most decisive ideal factor leading to the secularization of the West, according to Berger, was the process of 'rationalization'. This is a concept first developed by the German sociologist Max Weber in his book *The Protestant Ethic and the Spirit of Capitalism* in which he writes about the development of capitalism in England. Here he argues that a key aspect of the development of capitalism in Western Europe was the 'disenchantment of the world' in which rationality takes the place of mysticism in our understanding of the world. According to Weber, social action guided by rationality can lead to the organization of society on completely different lines from societies in which people are guided by tradition and superstition. For Weber, modern capitalism could not have developed without guidelines which were esentially rational, such as accounting and modern production techniques. Traditional ways of thinking are typically suspicious of such things. The result of this process of rational-ization in England was a new set of attitudes towards the world and the emergence of what Weber called 'the spirit of capitalism'.

The spirit of capitalism

Weber traces the origin of the spirit of capitalism back to the Reformation, from which Protestantism and the 'Protestant ethic' emerged. Protestantism contained within it the idea of the *calling* which sees all worldly pursuits and activities as created by God to be performed in the spirit of worship. The calling of the individual is to carry out all worldly activities to the best of his or her abilities in a moral and Christian manner. Protestantism, or rather Calvinism, and later sects such as Quakers and Pietists, contained doctrines which to some extent influenced the individual in his or her economic activities, and Weber shows that historically many of the early centres of capitalism were strongly Protestant. Weber does not claim that Calvinism is the source of rationalism, but that certain ideas of Calvinism caused its adherents to behave in a way which made them accumulate wealth in a systematic manner. A further characteristic of Calvinism is a rejection of mysticism and magical forms of salvation such as confession, penance and the intercession of saints. It was only a belief in the ultimate grace and mercy of God that became the precarious foundation of the plausibility of Christianity which, in an increasingly rational world, becomes more and more difficult to sustain. According to Berger,

> This reality then became amenable to systematic, rational penetration, both in thought and in activity, which we associate with modern science and technology. A sky empty of angels becomes open to the intervention of the astronomer and, eventually, the astronaut.
>
> (Berger, *The Social Reality of Religion*, p. 118)

The conflict of belief systems

The process of rationalization has not been a smooth one and has encountered opposition by those who claim to be the legitimate and divinely appointed purveyors of truth, namely, the Church. The story of Galileo Galilei and how he came into conflict with official Church teaching is a classic example of a clash of views in which those who control 'official knowledge' are able to silence those who challenge it.

Galileo is generally thought to be one of the inventors of the scientific method and he tried to apply his methods of investigation to the study of the stars. Knowledge of the universe in the seventeenth century was based on pure faith in the Church and its teachings but Galileo proposed that the only way we can gain a proper understanding of the earth and its place in the solar system is by observation and experimentation. He had always believed that this was the only true test of scientific theory:

> I think that in discussion of physical problems we ought to begin not from the authority of scriptural passages, but from sense, experience and necessary demonstration. . . . Nor is God any less excellently revealed in Nature's actions than in the sacred statement of the Bible.
>
> (Quoted in J. Bronowski, *The Ascent of Man*, London, BBC Publications, 1973)

Galileo was advised by Pope Urban VIII not to pursue his theories any further as there could be no ultimate test of God's power and any attempt to construct one would be blasphemous. Nevertheless, in 1632 Galileo published his book *Dialogue on the Great World Systems* which outlined the Copernican theory that the world was not the centre of God's universe but was one of many planets revolving around the sun. The Pope was outraged and summoned Galileo to Rome to appear before the Inquisition.

The learned and scholarly atmosphere of the Inquisition's court in Rome belied the fact that these clerics were not prepared to be swayed by any scientific evidence, no matter how convincing. They had decided that Galileo was to recant, and certainly Galileo had no choice in the matter, for the Inquisition was renowned for its powers of persuasion. Galileo was not tortured but the threat had been made; there was no question of his resisting for he was an elderly man who knew only too well the horrors of the rack. One William Lithgow, an Englishman who had been tortured by the Spanish Inquisition in 1620, and survived, describes the experience:

> I was brought to the rack, then mounted on the top of it. My legs were drawn through the two sides of the three-planked

rack. A chord was tied about my ankles. As the levers bent forward, the main force of my knees against the two planks burst asunder and the sinews of my hams, and the lids of my knees were crushed. My eyes began to startle, my mouth to foam and froth, and my teeth to chatter like the doubling of a drummer's sticks. My lips were shivering, my groans were vehement, and blood sprang from my arms, broken sinews, hands and knees. Being loosed from these pinnacles of pain, I was hand-fast set on the floor, with this incessant imploration: 'Confess! Confess!'

(Quoted in Bronowski, *The Ascent of Man*)

Galileo's clash with the Church illustrates the conflict of two belief systems each claiming to hold the key to the truth. The different conceptions of the truth contained within these two belief systems led their respective adherents to see the world differently. The ideas of the Church prevailed on this occasion, but the onslaught on the Church continued, culminating in 1859 in the publication of Darwin's *Origin of Species*. In this book Darwin challenged some of the most strongly held beliefs of Victorian Christianity. His theory of evolution was revolutionary, not just for the scientific world, but also for the Church and its teachings.

Secularization, religious pluralism and transformation

The process of rationalization helped to pave the way for the scientific world view which brought about a widespread questioning of the authority of the Church and its idea of the truth. It may be that such attacks on the Church have led to a decline in the importance of institutionalized religion, and indeed recent studies show that fewer people either go to church or are members of the established Church (*Church Statistics*, 1983). Despite this, however, many people still believe in God. For example, in 1978 a Gallup Poll survey found that 76 per cent of the population of Britain believe in God and 57 per cent believe in heaven. For Berger such figures show that secularization does not lead to a decline in the importance of religion in people's lives but instead to the reduced credibility of Christianity in producing a comprehensive universe of meaning. Whereas before religion acted as an important agent of integration within society and legitimation of the existing social order, Berger claims that a new situation prevails in which a number of religious views of the world compete with one another for the allegiance of individuals. In this climate of scepticism and rationality religious groups must convincingly market themselves and their beliefs. The increasing number of sects and movements, such as the Moonies, attest to the fact that religious belief still thrives. Bryan Wilson, however, in his book *Religion in Sociological Perspective* (1982) sees this situation as potentially dangerous, for, whereas previously religion helped to maintain social order by providing a comprehensive explanation of the world and how to live our lives in terms of work, leisure and family life, today it no longer has this function as there are now a variety of religious groups each providing us with different views on how to live our lives. This lack of universal guidelines, according to Wilson, results in more crime, suicide, divorce and loneliness.

For Berger and Luckmann, in this new type of secular society religion has not lost its importance but is merely practised and expressed in a different way. The natural urge to make sense of the world ensures that individuals seek out the answers to their questions from among the alternative religions. Religion today, therefore, has undergone a process of *transformation* for, despite the obvious decline in the importance of the Church, religion as such remains strong in the personal lives of individuals.

If we accept Berger and Luckmann's claim that the sociology of knowledge cannot exist without the sociology of religion, then it is possible to describe both religion and science as belief systems, as each tries to satisfy our natural human urge to make sense of the world. Furthermore, religion and science are claimed by their adherents to be able to provide us with the 'truth', and each is supported and promoted by a community of experts. Some sociologists, however, although recognizing such similarities, are not convinced by Berger and Luckmann's argument. As **Roy Wallis** comments: 'Drawing attention to such similarities is worthwhile but not worth broadening the term religion so far as to incorporate ideologies which are opposed to it' (in *Student Encyclopedia of Sociology*, M. Mann (ed.), 1984).

5 The Sources of Knowledge in Society – Education

Introduction

As a source of knowledge the education system plays a pre-eminent role in Western society today. Schools act as important agents of secondary socialization during which the child learns and internalizes the cultural and scientific achievements of society. A pupil's success or failure in this system is very much dependent upon the use he or she makes of the knowledge taught in the classroom, and a 'successful' pupil is one who is able effectively to remember and reproduce such knowledge under examination conditions, the reward for which is a diploma or certificate which can be used as 'currency' in the job market. A 'failure' is usually one who has not been able to gain enough certificates of a sufficiently high standard.

In Britain today educationists have identified certain groups, such as children of the working class and those of West Indian origin, as being more prone to educational failure than others. In other words, they have not been as effective as 'the rest of society' in learning and internalizing what has come to be accepted as 'official knowledge'. The aim of sociologists has been to explain why certain pupils 'fail' and others 'succeed', despite similarities in measured intelligence.

Early attempts to explain educational failure

A number of studies during the 1950s and 1960s, such as the *Early Leaving Report* (1954), revealed that the tripartite system of education (so-called because it was made up of three different types of schools, grammar, secondary modern and technical high) was not providing working-class children with sufficient opportunities for upward social mobility and was in fact helping to perpetuate the more conservative and divisive aspects of the class system. Studies outside the school attempted to show how school failure is not just related to the type of school a child goes to but also the cultural and social aspects of working-class life. The notion of 'cultural deprivation' was introduced, which seemed to show that there was something about working-class culture which affected the chances of a child from this social class doing well at school – such as poor home conditions and lack of educational success among working-class parents.

The response of policy makers to these findings was to implement two related strategies, the first being the introduction of comprehensive education designed to provide equality of educational opportunity for all, and the second was the extension of nursery education and the implementation of 'compensatory education' programmes, both of which it was hoped would counteract the effects of working-class culture. Compensatory education involved the setting up of Educational Priority Areas (EPAs) which would be provided with extra money and resources for equipment, buildings and teachers.

Despite these policies the statistics showed a continuing consistency in the under-achievement of working-class children.

Crisis in the sociology of education

The theoretical position of most sociologists concerned with education during this time was essentially functionalist, describing education as having both a socializing function and a means of selecting and allocating people to their appropriate roles in society. It was generally believed that an efficient education system would select people, regardless of their class background, and ensure that they were rewarded with jobs appropriate to their talents. It was abundantly evident, however, that the educational system was not functioning as expected.

The new sociology of education

Frustrated with the failure of the education system, a small group of sociologists began to question the basic assumptions on which they had relied for so long. Their focus of attention became the school curriculum and the assumption that working-class children were in some way deprived. With the publication in 1971 of *Knowledge and Control: New Directions for the Sociology of Education*, edited by **M. F. D. Young**, the debate was thrown wide open. Although the various authors who contributed to the book had their own different perspectives, there was one thing on which they were all agreed: that is, that the sociology of education must be considered as part of the sociology of knowledge. The theme running through the book was the notion that we cannot take for granted the knowledge taught in schools but must subject it to the most detailed theoretical and empirical investigation. For Young this means that sociologists must question generally accepted ideas and labels such as 'failure' and 'success' rather than take them for granted as they are defined by educationists.

M. F. D. Young

In his contributions to the book Young outlines the approach taken by the new sociology of education. He starts from the assumption that the image of society which we have is socially constructed and maintained by the interaction between individuals. This interactionist perspective is much influenced by Berger, Luckmann and Schutz, who argue that knowledge at all levels is a human product. For Young this would include educational knowledge, and he argues that the sociologist should be concerned with how knowledge is produced, supported and distributed through educational institutions.

Young proposes that we question all generally accepted definitions of reality, how they have become dominant and in whose interest they are maintained. For example, why is it that certain subjects have more status than others? In Britain it can be seen how certain academic disciplines such as English Literature, History and Mathematics have higher status than more practical subjects such as Home Economics or Woodwork. This has obvious significance for the way in which teachers *define* the abilities of their pupils. An 'intelligent' pupil, for example, is generally viewed as one who has an aptitude for academic subjects rather than more practical ones. He argues that in every society there is a group of people who dictate what should or should not be considered valid or high-status knowledge. As an example, he uses the work of Weber to demonstrate how in ancient China the nation's administrators defined a 'clever' person as one who had a knowledge of the classical Confucian texts. Such knowledge had no particular application other than being a means of getting into the civil service, which was the most highly regarded occupation.

For Young, the aim of the new sociology of education is to discover how knowledge becomes *stratified* – that is, divided into groups with higher and lower status.

Developments in the new sociology of education

In response to Young's exhortations there has been a whole range of studies investigating such issues as who controls the curriculum (**Bourdieu**, 1977), how a subject becomes an accepted part of the curriculum (**Goodson**, 1982), the 'hidden curriculum' (**Hargreaves**, 1982), and the role of language and culture in reproducing the patterns of failure in the education system (**Bernstein**, 1973).

Figure 5.1 **The hidden curriculum**
This refers to those things which a pupil learns along with official classroom subjects. He or she must acquire appropriate attitudes and behave in a particular way in order to gain the approval of teachers. It can be seen to operate in the way the school is organized – that is, in terms of its hierarchical nature, and also within the classroom.

The hidden curriculum transmits important messages with regard to the appropriate attitudes, such as the importance of obedience to superiors, co-operation and the virtues of hard work. It also teaches children their appropriate sex roles. In her study *Feminism and Science Teaching* (1981) **Judy Samuel** shows how the language and illustrations of science textbooks reinforce traditional sex roles. For example, physics and chemistry books refer to pupils exclusively as *he* and emphasize the masculinity of the subjects in their illustrations, which invariably show boys doing experiments. For some sociologists, learning the hidden curriculum can be seen as just as important as learning the official curriculum.

Bernstein and the significance of language

B. Bernstein has made an extremely important contribution to our understanding of the connection between language, class and educational achievement (*Class, Codes and Control*, vols. 1–3, 1971, 1973, 1975). From his research on working-class children in the classroom he found that they had difficulty coping with the formal language used by the teacher. Rejecting the usual labels attached to such children, he decided that they must be using a different kind of *linguistic code*, for their middle-class peers seemed to have little trouble coming to terms with the linguistic requirements of the school. In fact, all activities in the school are conducted in a certain formal way – in communicating with the teacher, reading school textbooks, writing homework and examinations.

From this he developed the idea of the 'elaborated' and 'restricted' codes. The latter is a form of speech which tends to be used in informal situations and assumes that those communicating have much in common in terms of experience and outlook. For this reason a good deal which is left unspoken is none the less recognized and understood by the speakers. Conversation tends to be restricted to description and narrative rather than to the abstract, mainly because the speaker feels that the listener will know what he or she is trying to say. For example, the phrase 'you know what I mean', is a typical figure of speech employed by those using the restricted code. The elaborated code, on the other hand, assumes much less and is, therefore, more complex in its structure and use of words. It also tends to be more analytical and abstract without taking for granted a common understanding of meaning between the speakers.

According to Bernstein, these codes are the products of different class situations. The restricted code originates within the working class in which the shared life-style of working people in terms of occupation, status and area of residence produce little opportunity for intellectual pursuits and a person is admired for his or her 'plain speaking' rather than for being verbose. The elaborated code arises from a culture which emphasizes the individual rather than the community and where the life-style and occupations of those involved promote the virtues of, and indeed demand, an intellectual and analytic approach to life. This, of course, refers to the middle class.

It should be emphasized, however, that Bernstein is not saying that the elaborated code is used exclusively by the middle class and the restricted code by the working class but that the culture of each class favours a particular language code. In explaining the origins of these linguistic codes Bernstein also examines the part played by the family. He claims that the way a person's role and status in the family is defined has a great deal of influence on the type of language used by the family member. Two types of family role systems are identified. The first of these is the 'positional family', in which a person is treated and acts in accordance with their formal status in the family – for example, father, mother, child. The means of communication, again, is based on an individual's position in the family and does not encourage references to individual differences. Control relies on the relative power of the member involved rather than as the result of negotiation. Thus, a child is expected to obey his or her father because he is *obliged* to do so. The second system, the 'person-oriented family', is that in which decisions are made and control is maintained through verbal negotiation. The status of the individual in the family is not used to enforce conformity but discussion of individual differences is encouraged.

From his research Bernstein tries to show that there is a connection between the working-class positional family and the restricted code and the middle-class, person-oriented family and the elaborated code. The relationship between educational performance and linguistic codes, put simply, is one in which working-class children who are socialized in an environment where the restricted code predominates may find it difficult to adjust to the linguistic requirements of the school (see Figure 5.2).

Pierre Bourdieu

Educational and cultural inequality

Both Bernstein and Bourdieu take a similar position with regard to the existence of differences between the language and culture of the school and that of the working class. They also agree that the way in which the culture is reproduced and passed on through the education system has a great deal to do with the power relations of the class system. In his book *Cultural Reproduction*

Figure 5.2 **Is working-class language deficient?**
This is a subject which has been debated at length, and some critics of Bernstein argue that he seems to imply that working-class language and thought is in some way inferior to that of the middle class. Bernstein denies such accusations, claiming that he does not see it as a situation in which one type of speech can be seen as superior to another; rather, it should be accepted that they are just different. The work of **William Labov** is often used to illustrate this. Labov found that lower-class black Americans are no less capable of expressing complex ideas than middle-class black Americans; the problem is that the non-standard English used by lower-class blacks is perceived to be inferior by their teachers. If this is the case, then the issue can be reversed and criticism can be made of schools and the education system for not recognizing the value of working-class speech patterns and for trying to teach such children to speak 'properly' through programmes of compensatory education. In fact, Bernstein has criticized such policies, and in 1969 he wrote a paper urging schools to accept rather than reject the working-class culture of their pupils.

(1977), Bourdieu and his colleague **J. Passeron** examine the process whereby the knowledge, ideas and beliefs of a society are reproduced. In doing this Bourdieu employs the concept of 'symbolic violence'. This means that certain classes in society are able to impose their meanings on the rest of society and thereby to exert their power, for by defining what is important to know and how to think they have an effective means of controlling the population.

This is not to say that the culture of the dominant class is superior to that of the subordinate class, but that having defined its own culture as superior and institutionalized it through the schools, the dominated class comes to see its own culture as being of less value than that of the dominant class. As Bourdieu is writing about French society he describes the dominant classes in France as the industrialists, professionals and executives, and subordinate classes as the workers, peasants and *petit bourgeoisie*. When the former groups enter school they are usually well

equipped linguistically and culturally to cope with the requirements of the school. They are, in the words of Bourdieu, rich in
'cultural capital'. The latter group, however, does not possess
such cultural capital, and when they enter school they are placed
at a disadvantage. This difference between the culture of the home
and the school is a key factor in reproducing class inequalities,
according to Bourdieu.

For Bourdieu, as for Bernstein, the language and culture which
a pupil brings to school are crucial factors which influence a
child's performance in the educational system. The problem thus
becomes not one of the 'culturally deprived' child, but one of a
system of stratification in which powerful groups are able to
impose their definitions of what is important knowledge on the
rest of society.

The problem of change

Bourdieu's theory is compelling, but there seems to be little scope
for an explanation of social change. Indeed, the prospect of the
individual's breaking away from the structural constraints of the
social system is minimal. This is in fact a recurring problem for
structuralist theories, which tend to be devoid of any analysis of
human consciousness. For Bourdieu, the way in which these
social and cultural inequalities might possibly be eliminated is
through a change in the class structure brought about by a transformation of the economic system. However, there is little in his
theory to show how this might be achieved.

Nell Keddie

The teacher and classroom knowledge

Further interesting research on the curriculum and school knowledge was carried out by **Nell Keddie** who, in her article 'Classroom Knowledge' (1971), investigates the method adopted by
teachers in the humanities department of a comprehensive school
to categorize pupils as 'able' or 'dull'. The teachers in this department did not agree with the teaching methods of the rest of the
staff who segregated pupils according to ability (streaming),
arguing that all pupils should be taught in the same way using

a common syllabus. To this end they introduced a new Mode 3 CSE which was based on course work, in which the pupils could investigate topics at their own pace. However, despite their rejection of streaming, Keddie found that the teachers soon began to treat the high-ability 'A' streamers in a different way from the low-ability 'C' streamers. For example, 'A'-stream pupils were thought to be able to deal with topics much more quickly than 'C'-stream pupils and could deal with abstract ideas very easily without needing illustrative examples, whereas 'C'-stream pupils were seen as only capable of understanding simple ideas.

The teachers, therefore, treated the pupils differently, and when 'C' streamers asked questions in the classroom it was seen as disruptive rather than intelligent behaviour. 'A' streamers, on the other hand, tended to accept the teachers' definition of what is important knowledge, and this is to a great extent a reason for their educational success.

According to Keddie, the problem is not one in which 'lower-ability' pupils are in some way culturally deprived but that the school and teachers do not accept as valid the cultural background of certain groups of children and, therefore, define them as 'deprived'. In a book edited by Keddie entitled *Tinker Taylor . . . The Myth of Cultural Deprivation* (1973) the idea that working-class and black cultures are in some way deprived is examined

Figure 5.3 **Thinking among the Trukese**
A cross-cultural study by **T. Gladwin** entitled 'Culture and Logical Process' (1973) in Keddie's book shows how a group of Pacific islanders known as the Trukese are able to navigate the waters around their island with a great skill without the use of a compass or charts. Through a combination of audio-visual skills and memory they are able to find their way from one island to the next which may be hundreds of miles away. Yet if the Trukese navigator were to be given a Western intelligence test he would probably fail it because his skills do not correspond with our idea of intelligence.

Such studies show that people develop different styles of thought to cope with their particular cultural and social environments.

further. She claims that their culture is not inferior; it is just different. Thus different cultures have different ways of thinking and applying their knowledge to solve problems. What for us in the West may be considered an inferior way of thinking may elsewhere be highly regarded.

Further developments

Studies have also been carried out on the school curriculum and in particular on the way in which certain subjects are taught and how they can be seen to support and legitimate the existing social order.

In an interesting analysis of music teaching in schools entitled *Music in Secondary Schools* (1972), **G. Vulliamy** shows how this subject was first introduced into the classroom as an important means of teaching moral and religious values and for this reason most music classes were confined to singing. By the 1920s and thirties an understanding and appreciation of 'good' music was required. By 'good' music Vulliamy means music 'in the European serious tradition', such as classical and orchestral music. Popular music tends to be looked down upon by music educators, and, despite various attempts to introduce it into the music curriculum, the emphasis has still been on traditional classical music.

Vulliamy points to the glaring absence of Afro-American music from most academic courses despite its great influence on twentieth-century Western music. Jazz, blues and rock, for example, all have their origins in the Afro-American tradition, and the music critic Henry Pleasants – himself taught in the 'classical tradition' – claims that music historians will see the twentieth century as one dominated by Afro-American music in the same way that one might associate the baroque period with Italian music. Nevertheless, rock, reggae, jazz and so on tend to be associated with lower status groups in society such as West Indians, and are not considered to be 'serious' music.

Vulliamy uses Bourdieu's idea of 'symbolic violence' to describe this process, for certain powerful groups are able to impose their ideas about valuable or high status knowledge and define the knowledge of other groups as inferior or worthless.

Conclusion

The new sociology of education indicates a number of interesting ways of approaching such issues as cultural deprivation and educational failure. It also encourages us to take a second look at the categories of knowledge which we take for granted. However, by defining all forms of knowledge as relative, the proponents of the new sociology of education provided very few guidelines as to what kinds of knowledge are valuable or useful. If there is no such thing as *true* or *objective* knowledge, then how can we judge the value or worth of anything, including the knowledge produced by the new sociology of education? This is significant for, despite the critical insights provided by the adherents to this school of thought, they offer few, if any, practical solutions to the problem which they identify. For example, how can teachers teach without imposing certain types of cultural outlook on their pupils? Some sociologists would argue that certain types of knowledge *are* more important than others, and there is no doubt that in modern industrial society certain skills and disciplines, such as literacy and numeracy, are essential if progress is to be made.

PART 3

Statistics and documentary readings

6 Statistics

Introduction

To a great extent the knowledge and image we hold of modern industrial Britain are a result of the vast amount of statistical information we come across in the media and official reports produced by the government. Almost every day we can read newspaper headlines such as those shown below.

Mail on Sunday,
13 March 1983

The Financial Times, 17 Oct. 1986

From these various statistical images a composite picture of British society emerges, one of the most authoritative of which is that presented by the Central Statistical Office which represents the official government view.

- There were 56 million people living in the United Kingdom in 1983.
- Almost 90 per cent of people in England and Wales lived in urban areas in 1981.
- The number of people aged 65 or over in the United Kingdom has increased by over 2 million since 1961. They now make up 16 per cent of the population.
- The proportion of people living in one-parent families with dependent children has doubled since 1961 from 2.5 per cent in Great Britain.
- 47 per cent of people aged 75 or over lived alone in 1983.
- Average household size fell from 3.1 in 1961 to 2.6 in 1983.
- There were 162,000 divorces in the United Kingdom in 1983; about 20 per cent of those in England and Wales involved at least one partner who had been divorced before, compared with only 9 per cent in 1971.

(*Social Trends* 15, London, HMSO, 1985.)

This short extract from the Introduction to *Social Trends* 15, 1985, published by the government, gives a small glimpse of Britain in the mid-1980s. It goes on to present the nation's vital statistics, including everything from our general health to the distribution of wealth. Social statistics, then, are social knowledge in mathematical form which present a picture of the changing structure of society.

Official statistics and power

Collecting social statistics, however, is not merely an academic exercise, neither are they read out of pure interest. They are, in fact, the raw materials which governments use to build their policies, and without them governments would be unable to make decisions on questions such as how many schools to build or how many doctors to train. On the basis of existing data policy makers are able to make projections about the future needs of society.

Governments have for centuries used statistics for official purposes, and the census, which involves the collection of information on the size of the population as well as economic and social data about all the people within a country, goes back to biblical times when King Herod conducted a census at the time of Christ's birth. Initially, such information was gathered for the purposes of conscription and taxation. Kings such as William I of England who was responsible for the Domesday Book (1066–1087) wanted to know how many people could be taxed and how much each could pay and also how many able-bodied men there were in the population who could be called upon to fight for their king.

Despite the fact that today the amount of data collected by the statistical departments of governments has become much greater and the statistical techniques involved are much more complex, it is still true that for those who control them official statistics are a source of *power*. By withholding information or releasing it selectively, governments are able to confound their opponents and influence the population's perceptions of the country's social and economic performance. Moreover, because governments control the agencies responsible for data collection, which in Britain is called the Government Statistical Service, they are also able to influence the way in which official statistics are gathered.

As sources of knowledge, therefore, official statistics should be treated with the greatest caution, for they, like many other forms of knowledge, are *socially constructed*. Factual information may exist 'out there' in society, but what is selected from this vast ocean of facts and how they are measured to a great extent reflect the choices and priorities of those with power. A group of government statisticians describe this process in the following way:

> The methods and concepts developed and used for official statistics are shaped by the sorts of policies powerful people in the state wish to consider and by the concerns which preoccupy them. These concerns determine, at least partly, which phenomena are to be investigated as 'social problems' and which are neglected.
> (J. Irvine, I. Miles and J. Evans (eds), *Demystifying Social Statistics*, London, Pluto Press, 1979)

The production of social statistics

Official statistics and social statistics in general are, therefore, social products which are the result of a number of processes each of which will affect the end product. Production takes place at two distinct levels. Firstly, the *conceptual level* involves decisions on the part of sponsoring bodies such as the state as to how a particular social problem is to be defined and the priority it is to be given. This sets the tone of the research. Secondly, there is the *technical level* – that is, the collection process itself. This begins with the government statisticians working out how to *operationalize*, that is, put into mathematical terms, the problems identified by their superiors. This means that they have to frame them in such a way that they can be measured mathematically. For example, if we are to measure poverty we must have a definition which can be put into numerical form and used as a standard against which we can judge those being investigated. The administration and analysis of official statistics is supervised by a number of support staff such as clerks and computer operators. This process too can have a significant effect on the results. We will now examine each of these levels in a little more detail.

(A) The conceptual level

In planning a piece of statistical research a statistician will categorize people or things according to certain criteria. As people are infinitely complicated and different this can involve, for the purposes of convenience, limiting the number of possible categories, or restricting them in some way. This is itself a creative process, though the statistician will to a greater or lesser extent be influenced by the guidelines issued by his or her superiors'. It is at this point that decisions are made as to who is and who is not to be included in the research, and this can significantly influence the outcome of the research. Let us take as our example government unemployment figures.

UNEMPLOYMENT STATISTICS
Unemployment figures are an important indicator of a country's economic performance as well as of the effectiveness of a government's economic policies. At a personal level also, unemployment involves a great deal of financial and emotional hardship. In May

1987 unemployment in Britain stood at about 3.1 million which was approxiately 11 per cent of the working population. Adrian Sinfield and Neil Fraser (*The Real Cost of Unemployment*, 1985) estimated that the cost to the government of over 13 per cent unemployment is about £20,000 million. This is calculated on the basis of losses to government revenues such as income tax, National Insurance contributions and also the cost of unemployment and other benefits.

For these reasons governments are most concerned with the level of unemployment and estimating future trends. Not everyone, however, agrees with the government's estimates, and in Britain left-wing critics of Mrs Thatcher's government claim that it greatly under-estimates the true extent of unemployment. There are also those right-wing critics of the government who claim that official figures actually exaggerate the 'true' level of unemployment. The reason for this disagreement is mainly due to the way in which unemployment is *defined*.

MEASURING UNEMPLOYMENT

In 1979 unemployment statistics were based on monthly returns from all the unemployment exchanges in the country, giving the total number of people who 'signed on' for unemployment and other benefits. Eligibility for benefits, however, was an important reason for 'signing on', and as certain groups, such as women with working husbands, were often not eligible for unemployment benefit or social security benefits they tended not to sign on. Some critics of the government's methods of counting argue that these non-claimers should also be included in the figures on unemployment. This exclusion of non-claimants still stands today, the largest single group being women. In her article 'Women and Society' (1985) Sarah Fildes estimate that 'the numbers of women who say they are looking for a job who are excluded from the figures range from a half to a third of the official total'.

CHANGES IN THE OFFICIAL DEFINITION OF UNEMPLOYMENT

After 1979 a number of changes were made in the way in which unemployment was measured. In 1987 unemployment was calculated on the basis of those actually claiming benefit as opposed to the numbers registering at unemployment exchanges. This method of measuring unemployment, according to *Employment*

Gazette (12 December 1983) removed approximately 189,000 from the total. Furthermore, the government excluded 'school leavers' from the figures until the September after leaving school when they became eligible, and even then it only included those who actually claimed. According to M. Denscombe in *Sociology Update* (1984) this reduced the official count by some 168,000.

Another change took place in October 1983 when the government ruled that unemployed men over the age of sixty were no longer required to 'sign on' in order to receive certain long-term benefits. As a result a large number of unemployed men over sixty years of age were deleted from the unemployment figures. In April 1986 the government made a further change in the method of counting the unemployed when it decided to delay the count by two weeks in order to allow those who had found work to de-register. This was because ministers reckoned that, although the newly unemployed register for benefit immediately, those who find jobs tend to delay in informing the Department of Employment.

Since 1979 there have been six changes to the method of counting the unemployed and left-wing critics of the government such as P. Townsend estimated the true level of unemployment to be over 5 million (*News on Sunday*, 17 May 1987). Right-wing commentators, however, estimate that the government figures exaggerate the level of unemployment. They claim that a large number of those receiving unemployment benefit are not actually looking for work or already have a job but do not declare it. They also claim that as many as 352,000 people are 'job changers' and are only out of work for four weeks or less (Denscombe, *Sociology Update*, 1987). Finally, right-wing critics argue that the unemployable claimants, such as the severely mentally handicapped and physically disabled, should not be counted. They estimate the 'true' level of unemployment to be only about 2.3 million (M. Slattery, *Official Statistics*, 1986).

As we can see from the example of unemployment, the 'official picture' of society presented by the government can vary not necessarily because of actual changes in society or the economy but because of the changing *definitions* of the situation by the state. The *validity* of such official statistics is thus brought into question.

(B) The technical level

During the collection process statistical data pass through a number of channels, and these in turn can have an effect on the final product. Data which the government statistical departments receive come primarily from official forms which various people and organizations are required to fill in. Businesses, for example, are requested to co-operate in providing honest and truthful data. However, as a group of government statisticians point out, many companies falsify or neglect to provide data. To illustrate their point they quote a correspondent who wrote:

> I was pressed time and time again to use false figures for turn-over, cost of raw materials, etc for fear of the taxman. They did not realize that the taxman would never see the forms – or so I hoped. I fought bitter battles and once threatened to give notice to prevent fraud. I know that others do not have the power to do this or do not care.'
>
> (Irvine, Miles and Evans (eds), *Demystifying Social Statistics*)

Once these data reach the government department concerned they are sorted and collated by clerical workers who tend to be the least knowledgeable and experienced of the staff. The work is not only boring but also requires initiative as anomalies often arise which need to be dealt with properly. Although clerical workers are required to refer all anomalies to their supervisors, it often requires experience and knowledge to recognize when something needs further attention. This can often lead to erroneous information being fed into the computer and eventually ending up in published reports. This problem would not be so great if it occurred only rarely but, as the government statisticians quoted above claim, there is no telling exactly how widespread it is:

> From the time when figures are first entered on a form in a local Government or business office, until the statistics are published in statistical volumes and reports, data processing is highly sensitive to many mundane sources of error – misunderstood instructions on forms, misreading of hastily written figures, misplacing a decimal point, losing one's place in copying, accidental 'corruption' of data in computer files, or printing

errors. It is quite possible for a mistake anywhere along the line to go undetected and work its way through into published figures.

(Irvine, Miles and Evans (eds), *Demystifying Social Statistics*)

Such problems involved in the collection and processing of statistical data raise serious questions as to the *reliability* of official statistics.

Positivism and statistics

Despite these problems, however, the positivists argue that an accurate and objective picture of society can be drawn with the use of statistics. Durkheim, for example, claimed that we must 'consider social facts as things'. By this he meant that there is a social reality in the world which, through objective scientific investigation, can be made known. In his famous study of suicide (1897) Durkheim relied heavily on statistical data collected from a number of European countries and used them as the basis for his scientific explanation of suicide. Many researchers including positivists have pointed to the faults in Durkheim's study. The reliability of his statistics, for example, has been questioned, particularly as the collection of such information at the turn of the century was unsystematic and often lacked medical corroboration. Nevertheless, the positivists argue that what is needed is a sharpening of the tools involved in data collection, for in principle they believe that such phenomena as the suicide rate or the rate of unemployment can be accurately measured.

Phenomenology and statistics

Phenomenologists would question the view that we are able to objectively measure social reality – even if it does exist. This is because reality, as perceived by individuals, is *constructed*. In the process of interaction people actively select and choose from the vast amount of information they receive. What they decide to choose depends upon expectations they have and the meanings they attach to a particular situation. Official statistics, then, are ultimately specific representations of reality and reflect the choices

Table 6.1 UK unemployed claimants: by sex, age, and duration, April 1984 (percentages and thousands)

	Duration of unemployment (weeks)						total (= 100%) (thousands)
	Up to 2	Over 2, up to 8	Over 8 up to 26	Over 26, up to 52	Over 52, up to 104	Over 104	
Males aged:							
16–19	5.8	12.8	28.0	29.4	18.8	5.1	307.1
20–24	5.2	10.9	23.9	20.5	18.6	20.9	418.6
25–34	4.6	9.8	21.6	17.8	19.2	27.0	503.1
35–49	4.3	8.8	19.6	16.4	19.1	31.8	493.2
50–59	3.6	6.5	16.9	17.3	20.5	35.3	368.5
60 or over	6.6	9.9	28.0	32.6	11.4	11.4	89.6
All males aged 16 or over	4.7	9.7	22.0	20.1	18.9	24.6	2,180.1
Females aged:							
16–19	5.9	12.8	29.8	30.4	17.1	4.1	222.2
20–24	6.2	12.8	29.0	24.7	14.2	13.0	232.7
25–34	6.5	13.7	30.9	27.4	12.9	8.6	208.4
35–49	6.2	12.3	25.4	22.5	17.9	15.7	147.2
50 or over	3.3	6.5	16.3	18.4	22.0	33.5	117.2
All females aged 16 or over	5.8	12.1	27.5	25.5	16.2	12.9	927.6

Source: Department of Employment, Social Trends, 15, 1985.

made by the state in the process of constructing an 'official' view of reality. Unemployment statistics, therefore, according to phenomenologists, show us nothing more than the way the government defines unemployment (usually for its own convenience).

Despite the merits of their argument, the phenomenologists seem to be advising us to do no quantitative research at all and that statistics are little more than useless, but there is no doubt that policy makers and planners would be unable to do their jobs at all without numerical data.

Discussion questions on statistics

1 Try to draw a statistical picture of the members of your class by dividing them up into such categories as (a) age, (b) sex, (c) race, (d) class, (e) religious belief, (f) musical taste. Make a note of the problems you encounter in trying to classify people.
2 In view of the fact that not everyone agrees with the way in which the government defines unemployment, study Table 6.1 on p. 63 and, on the basis of what S. Fildes says on p. 59, try to estimate how many unemployed women there might actually be.
3 In view of the criticisms of statistics made by the phenomenologists, and the problems involved in their collection, could it be said that official statistics are 'useless'?

7 Documentary readings

The following readings are extracts from the works of both sociologists and non-sociologists which address some of the issues raised in this volume. The first three readings are concerned with some of the ideas which have played an important part in the development of the sociology of knowledge, such as *ideology* and *hegemony*. Readings 4 and 5 are about the works of K. Mannheim and Berger and Luckmann, who have written classics in the field. The remaining extracts are concerned with specific issues such as the nature of scientific knowledge and the role of religion in society.

Origins of the sociology of knowledge

The sociology of knowledge is only a recent development and is the result of attempts by sociologists to discover how particular *world views* emerge from the society in which they are located. It is in the work of Marx and Durkheim that we find the first systematic attempts at a sociological explanation of the relationship between knowledge and society.

Marx and the sociology of knowledge

According to Marx, all ideas and knowledge in society have their origins in the material conditions of life. **Russell Keat** and **John Urry** summarize Marx's theory in the first extract.

Reading 1   Marx and the origins of knowledge

Essentially, for Marx the manner in which knowledge is produced in a society, and its content, are directly related to the social relations of material production. For Marx, the class which is the ruling material force in a society also has control over the means of mental production. The ruling ideas are those held by the ruling class. Such ideas represent in an ideal form the social relations of production. There are two central and connected elements in Marx's concept of ideology. First, a specification of particular forms of distortion are dependent upon the relations of material production. In particular, it is held that the acceptance of ideologically distorted beliefs serve the *interests* of specific social classes. It is not that the ruling class intentionally and conspiratorially aims to dominate ideologically, rather that the structure of social relationships systematically generates ideological distortions which serve the class-interests of the dominant class.

(R. Keat and J. Urry, *Social Theory as Science*, London, Routledge and Kegan Paul, 1975, p. 177)

Recent Marxists have examined how the bourgeoisie is able to maintain its position of ideological dominance over the subordinate classes. In trying to explain how the ruling class maintains its position of power, especially in the Western democracies, Gramsci developed the idea of *hegemony*. This involves the ruling class gaining the active consent of the rest of society not only for the way it rules but also for the way it sees the world. In the next extract, **Peter Musgrave** gives an explanation of how the term 'hegemony' is used today.

Reading 2   Hegemony

It is now commonly used to indicate a state of consensual predominance of the powerful group or class in a society or social system over the ruled. It covers the whole range of norms and values, not just the political, involved in the ruling group's view of the world. A ruling class or group to which legitimacy is given has achieved hegemony; its rule is accepted without question and alternatives are not mooted. A hegemonic class imposes its own view on society as a whole.

(P. Musgrave in *The Macmillan Student Encyclopedia of Sociology*, M. Mann (ed.), London, Macmillan, 1984, p. 154)

Discussion questions

1 What do you understand by the term 'ideology'? Illustrate your

answer by giving examples from specific social systems, e.g.,
fendalism.
2 How does Marx explain the origin of knowledge and ideas in
   society?
3 In what way is Gramsci's theory of hegemony a development
   of Marx's concept of ideology?

Karl Mannheim

Karl Mannheim was one of the first sociologists to write
specifically on the sociology of knowledge. Like Marx, he points
to the fact that the ideas and beliefs of a particular group in society
is very much dependent on its class position. For Mannheim all
knowledge is ideological, and he sees the sociology of knowledge
as a means of synthesizing all the competing ideologies. The one
group in society able to do this, he claims, is the free-floating
intelligentsia who, because they are relatively unaffected by class
interests, are able to see and understand all points of view, as P.
Hamilton points out in the next extract.

Reading 3   Mannheim's sociology of knowledge

Mannheim saw a relatively classless European intellectual elite
as providing the source of a 'dynamic mediation' between both
left and right political blocs: the terms under which such a
mediation could be achieved, the erection of a 'science of
politics' were to be accomplished by Mannheim's relationist
sociology of knowledge. It is important to note that Mannheim
does set a specific limit on the sociology of knowledge which
gravely impairs the possibility of its achieving scientific status;
it is to deal wholly with *ideologies* (e.g. including both
conservative *ideology* and radical *utopia*) for it is to be the means
of a resolution of ideological conflict. The focus of Mannheim's
work is then ideology, and sociology of knowledge is the
means by which ideologies are investigated. The definition of
non-scientific knowledge is that it is socially limited by its
contextual location (apart of course from that available to the
intellectual elite) to being simply a representation of the
interests and values of the group which holds it; it is true for

them only, and there is no way in which its general validity can be judged, since no general social context exists.
(P. Hamilton, *Knowledge and Social Structure*, London, Routledge and Kegan Paul, 1974, p. 121)

The social construction of reality

An important feature of early theories in the sociology of knowledge is that they have tended to be concerned with higher-level knowledge such as religious beliefs, political philosophies and ideologies. Despite Mannheim's attempt to discover 'how men actually think', his work has none the less also been concerned mainly with higher-level knowledge. It is in the work of Berger and Luckmann that the sociology of knowledge enters the realm of commonsense knowledge and everyday reality. In their book *The Social Construction of Reality* they argue that the sociology of knowledge should not just be concerned with *theoretical thought* but also with the *commonsense world of everyday life*. In an article written with Hansfried Kellner entitled 'Marriage and the construction of reality', Berger attempts to apply this idea to the way in which marital partners produce their reality and view of the world. In the next reading Margaret Poloma provides a summary of this study.

Reading 4   Marriage and the construction of reality

When two people marry each must attempt to correlate his/her respective realities with the other's. The marriage partner becomes the most important significant other for the spouse. Thus, the objective reality of marriage and the setting up of a new family is a product of the subjective dispositions of the bride and the groom; this objective reality also acts back on the couple, affecting their individual subjective realities. For example, marriage may mean the breaking off of old friendships established during singlehood for new friendships that can be jointly shared. Similar changes may take place in eating preferences, recreational activities, decorating choices, and so on. This is a gradual process that goes on throughout marriage.

Conversation or 'talking through' issues is the main device

through which the new world view is constructed in marriage. Each partner contributes from his or her subjective reality views that are 'hashed over' in conversation. These discussions from furniture style preferences to the number of desired children become part of an objective reality that acts back on the married couple. For example, a young woman may have been very uninterested in politics before her marriage. As her husband continues to voice his interests in local political affairs, she may come to identify herself as a political liberal, sharing his views. Similarly, she may more clearly define herself as an antique furniture buff who appreciates classical music, also reflecting her husband's tastes. This same process is also occurring with the husband as he develops an interest in ballet and an appreciation of medieval art because of his wife's influence. Two distinct biographies are aired in conversations, and redefinitions occur that will permit the new definitions to be included in the shared reality of marriage.

(Margaret M. Poloma, *Contemporary Sociological Theories*, New York, Macmillan, 1979, pp. 200–1)

Discussion questions

1 What, for Mannheim, should be the main focus of attention for the sociology of knowledge?
2 To what use can the sociology of knowledge be put, according to Mannheim?
3 In what way is the work of Berger and Luckmann different from previous theories in the sociology of knowledge?
4 Examine other areas of life and the way reality is created – e.g., in the mass media.

The sociology of science

The scientific method

Science is generally accepted to be a discipline which provides us with hard facts, and the knowledge it produces is a result of the objective pursuit of knowledge by a community of scientists dedicated to discovering the *truth* about the natural world.

Despite this desire to discover the truth, many philosophers of science would argue that this is an impossible dream because everything that scientists observe and discover is contaminated by their perceptions of the world and, therefore, no knowledge can be said to be pure. According to Karl Popper, the best we can hope for is to prove that a theory is wrong and that those theories which have not been disproved are used as the basis for further research. This approach to science is known as the hypothetico-deductive model and works on the principle of falsification. In the following extract **Stewart Richards** explains the main principles of this method.

Reading 5   *The method of falsification*

The most influential advocate of this conception of scientific methodology has been Karl Popper. His views were first published in 1934 in *The Logic of Scientific Discovery* (translated into English, 1959) but the title of his more recent book *Conjectures and Refutations* (1963), encapsulates the essentials of his 'method of falsification'. Hypotheses are to be developed and attempts made to falsify them through empirical research. In Popper's own words, '. . . there is no more rational procedure than the method of trial and error – of conjecture and refutation; of boldly proposing theories; of trying our best to show that these are erroneous and of accepting them tenta- tively if our critical efforts are unsuccessful.' . . . we can at any rate say that for the falsificationist a theory qualifies as part of tbe body of scientific knowledge by being falsifiable but not yet falsified. To say of a theory that it is falsifiable is to say that it has informative content and the more informative it is the more falsifiable it must be. The more falsifiable a theory is the better, so it is a scientist's job to advance 'bold conjec- tures' in preference to cautious ones.

(Stewart Richards, *Philosophy and Sociology of Science: An Introduction*, Oxford, Blackwell, 1983, pp. 52–5)

The scientific ethos

Early sociological studies of scientific knowledge took it for granted that this is how scientific progress is made, and functionalists such as R. K. Merton concentrated their research on the role of science as a subsystem in society and the social conditions necessary for scientists to do their work most effectively. Merton provides a set of *institutional imperatives*, which he calls the *ethos of science*, as the social principles upon which modern science should be founded. These are summarized in the next extract by Stewart Richards.

Reading 6   *The ethos of science*

Merton's first institutional imperative is that of *universalism*. The purpose of this is to guarantee that new knowledge is evaluated solely in terms of objective, impersonal criteria, and that such things as career advancement are determined solely by talent.

'*Communism*' is the second norm, intended in the sense that the 'goods' of science – its body of public knowledge – are subject, not to private, but to common or public ownership. Science accumulates knowledge by means of its extended, cooperative enterprise, its findings being assigned to the whole community. As a result, the only property rights of the individual scientist are those of recognition and esteem which accrue roughly in proportion to the importance of his work. It is for this reason that disputes over priority of discovery, a recurring phenomenon throughout the history of science, are seen as conforming entirely to the institutional imperatives. The right to be acknowledged for good work is absolute. Conversely, secrecy by the scientist is forbidden. . . .

Merton's third imperative element of the scientific ethos is that of *disinterestedness*, taken to mean a deep, but detached interest in the workings of the world, an interest that is, simply for its own sake. The scientist is expected to make his discoveries available for public scrutiny and there is, accordingly, little scope for fraud or irresponsibility. . . .

The final institutional imperative is what Merton calls *organised scepticism*. Clearly, this interrelates with the others and, indeed, is a crucial part of the scientific methodology itself. It is this element which most often brings science into conflict with other social institutions, such as the Church or the State, for science 'does not preserve the cleavage between the sacred and the profane, between that which requires uncritical respect and that which can be objectively analysed'.

(Richards, *Philosophy and Sociology of Science*, pp. 103–4)

Discussion questions

1 What are the main characteristics of the scientific method?
2 What are the main principles of the method of falsification?
3 Why does Merton see the ethos of science as being so important?

The new sociology of science

Historical evidence and recent events such as the Velikovsky affair have led philosophers and sociologists to question their previous assumptions about the way in which scientific progress occurs. This has resulted in a new sociology of science which is based on the idea that scientific knowledge, no less than other forms of knowledge, is a social product. K. Knorr-Cetina ('The Ethnographic Study of Scientific Work: Towards a Constructivist Interpretation of Science', 1983), for example, argues that scientists select and choose from the vast body of data available in the production of scientific knowledge. Gilbert and Mulkay illustrate this well in their paper 'Contexts of Scientific Discourse', in which they quote a scientist's views on the subject.

Reading 7   The scientist at work

It's appalling really, it's taught all the way in school, the notion that you make all these observations in a Darwinian sense. . . . That's just rubbish, this 'detached observation'. What do you see? Well, what do you see? God knows you see everything. And, in fact, you see what you *want* to see, for the most part. Or you see the choices between one or two rather narrow alternatives. That doesn't get admitted into the scientific literature. In fact, we write history all the time, a sort of hindsight. The order in which experiments are done. All manner of nonsense. So the personal side does get taken out of this sort of paper. Maybe it's felt that it isn't the place for it to be put. I don't know. . . . Sometimes you get more of the personal side in reviews. Some of them are quite scandalous actually, once you read between the lines.

(N. Gilbert and M. Mulkay, 'Contexts of Scientific Discourse' in *The Social Process of Scientific Investigation*, K. Knorr *et al.* (eds), Dordrecht, Netherlands, D. Reidel Publishing Co., 1980, p. 287)

The above quotation reveals how scientists actually construct scientific knowledge, and the way in which they select and put together this knowledge is very much dependent on the context in which the research is taking place or, as Knorr-Cetina calls it, the *contextual location* of the research. This refers to such things as the personal and professional views of the scientist, the pressure upon him or her to produce results and the level of competition from other scientists. All these vary over time and affect the production of scientific knowledge. K. Knorr-Cetina briefly summarizes this theory in the next extract.

Reading 8   *The context of scientific research*

This contextual location reveals that the products of scientific research are fabricated and negotiated by particular agents at a particular time and place; that these products are carved by the particular interests of these agents, and by local rather than universally valid interpretations; and that scientific actors play on the very limits of the situational location of their actions.

(K. Knorr-Cetina, *The Manufacture of Knowledge; An Essay on the Constructivist and Contextual Nature of Science*, Oxford, Pergamon, 1981, p. 58).

Scientific revolutions

It would seem that scientists are not the open-minded and objective observers of the natural world that they were thought to be. In fact, according to T. Kuhn, scientists tend to be very conservative in their outlook and are reluctant to see the natural world outside the restrictions of their particular *paradigm*. If this is the case then how is scientific progress made? According to Kuhn it is through *scientific revolutions* that science progresses and the way this occurs is summarized in the following extract by Stewart Richards.

Reading 9   Scientific revolution

That changes of paradigms occur at all may seem surprising in view of the sophisticated protectionist attitude within which normal science operates. Yet it is to the history of science that Kuhn appeals in arguing his theory and it is the revolutionary paradigm shifts which he identifies as the most important source of scientific 'advancement'. . . .

In the mature sciences psychological commitment by a community to its paradigms is enormously strong and it is for this reason that events leading to the fall of a paradigm, and to its replacement by one that is more comprehensive, are so traumatic, in much the same way as are political upheavals. New discovery, according to Kuhn, begins with the awareness of anomaly – that is that nature has in some way violated the expectations aroused by the paradigm. Because of the nature of normal science, the start of a revolutionary phase is at first resisted. The significance of the observed anomaly may be missed altogether, or at least it may be dismissed. The paradox associated with paradigm-shift is that genuine anomaly is acknowledged only when there *is* a detailed body of expectations from which it sticks out like the proverbial sore thumb. Without the 'received' background pattern, the unexpected result would not be seen.

(Richards, *Philosophy and Sociology of Science* pp. 62–3)

According to Kuhn there is not necessarily any connection between an existing paradigm and its predecessor, and this is because new paradigms emerge as a result of certain scientists thinking in ways completely different from what is expected. To this extent, Kuhn's theory is similar to Feyerabend's, in that both see scientific progress as being the result of processes which are not necessarily logical or rational. For example, Einstein's theory of relativity does not follow logically from Newton's mechanics. It required (initially, anyway) a sort of leap of faith on the part of the scientist trained within the Newtonian tradition. However, as Broad and Wade point out in the next extract, Feyerabend's position is much more extreme.

Reading 10   Anarchistic science

Feyerabend not only admits non-rational elements into the scientific process but sees them as dominant. Science, he says, is an ideology, completely shaped at any moment in time by its historical and cultural context. Scientific disputes are resolved not on their merits but by the theatrical and oratorical skills of their advocates, much as are legal cases. There is no one scientific method, good for all times and places, in fact, there is no such thing as a scientific method. Despite scientists' claims, the rule in science is that 'anything goes'.

(Broad and Wade, *Betrayers of the Truth*, p. 133)

Discussion questions

1 What is the theoretical perspective adopted by those in the new sociology of science?
2 What does Knorr-Cetina mean by the contextual location of scientists? What effect does this have on the production of scientific knowledge?
3 To what extent can it be said that the scientific community is conservative?
4 How does scientific progress occur? Is it primarily due to scientists adopting the method of falsification?

Education and the sociology of knowledge

Over the past decade a substantial contribution has been made by sociologists of knowledge to the sociology of education. Their main concern has been with the sort of knowledge children are taught at school and the development of the school curriculum. This has involved an analysis of what is taught both formally and informally in the school. Although there had been a few attempts to examine school knowledge during the 1960s, such as that by F. Musgrove in 1968, sociologists of education have tended to regard this area as none of their concern. It was in 1971 after the publication of *Knowledge and Control*, edited by M. F. D. Young, that school knowledge became a hotly debated subject among sociologists. In the next extract D. Gorbutt makes one of the first analyses of the impact of the new sociology of education.

Reading 11   The significance of the new sociology of education

The relativization of educational knowledge is implicit and explicit in several of the contributions to Michael F. D. Young's book *Knowledge and Control.* . . . As Young points out 'Treating "what we know" as problematic, in order that it becomes the object of enquiry, rather than as given, is difficult and perhaps nowhere more than in education. The out-thereness of the content of what is taught, whether it be as subjects, forms of enquiry, topics or ways of knowing, is very much part of the educator's taken for granted world'. . . . It is not surprising that treating knowledge in this way has excited more than a ripple of interest, particularly amongst philosophers of education, for the worthwhileness of particular educational activities can no longer be justified in absolute terms once the social basis of such justification is recognized. The apparent self-evident justification for education into particular forms of knowledge is laid bare as an ideological statement. The process through which particular curricula are institutionalized and justified becomes open to sociological examination. Thus, for example, the social assumptions underlying compensatory education, meaningful curricula for non-academic school leavers and mathematics for all can become the object of enquiry. We are forced into an often uncomfortable re-examination of the content and underlying assumptions of the curriculum at all levels.

(D. Gorbutt, 'The New Sociology of Education', in *Education for Teaching*, Autumn 1972, pp. 7–8)

There are several contributions to Young's book, and it would be reasonable to assume that there is no single view contained within it. Nevertheless, Young points to a common theme running through the book.

Reading 12   Knowledge and control – a common aim

Though it will be obvious to the reader that all contributors do not share a common doctrine or perspective, it would be true to say that what they all hold in common is that they do not take for granted existing definitions of educational reality, and therefore do 'make' rather than 'take' problems for the sociology of education. They are inevitably led to consider, often from widely different perspectives, 'what counts as educational knowledge' as problematic. The implication of this is that one major focus of the sociology of education becomes an enquiry into the social organisation of knowledge in educational institutions. Thus, and this has important implications for the organisation of sociological knowledge, sociology of education is no longer conceived as the area of enquiry distinct from the sociology of knowledge.

(M. F. D. Young, Introduction, *Knowledge and Control: New Directions in the Sociology of Education*, London, Collier-Macmillan, 1971, pp. 2–3)

The theoretical perspectives of the contributors to *Knowledge and Control*, therefore, differ despite their common aim. There is, for example, the structuralist Marxist approach of Pierre Bourdieu and the symbolic interactionist approach of Nell Keddie. In the following extract R. K. Brown summarizes the position of Bourdieu with particular reference to the role of education in the reproduction of the cultural system as well as the importance of *cultural capital*.

Reading 13   Cultural capital

It is to this continuity (or reproduction) of a class society that he directs his attention. He points out that the educational system (in this case France but the same would apply to England or Scotland) . . . demands a linguistic and cultural competence that it does not itself provide. This gives an advantage to those from families that diffusely and implicitly transmit the necessary 'instruments of appropriation of culture'. As a wealth of statistics show, an apparently open and meritocratic system is therefore predisposed to favour those who already have '*cultural capital*'. Possession of cultural capital is closely associated with possession of economic capital; Bourdieu's detailed examination of the French upper classes demonstrates, however, that the relationship between the two forms is complex: the distribution is not the same; cultural capital (i.e. academic qualifications) is most effective (outside the economic market) when combined with economic capital and political power; and in any case those with economic capital both have more chances of possessing cultural capital *and* are more able to do without it. There is thus value in considering cultural capital and its reproduction separately.

(R. K. Brown, Introduction, *Knowledge, Education and Cultural Change*, London, Tavistock Publications, 1973, p. 5)

Discussion questions

1 What is the main focus of attention of the new sociology of education?
2 Which theoretical perspectives are represented in the new sociology of education?
3 What factors do you think would come under the heading 'cultural capital'?

Recent developments in the new sociology of education

The book *Knowledge and Control* has led to research along the lines suggested by M. F. D. Young both in the field of the official curriculum and in the unofficial or hidden curriculum. With regard to the hidden curriculum there has been a good deal of research done on the messages which pupils receive about appropriate behaviour and attitudes. Particular reference can be made to studies of sex-role stereotyping and the way children at school are taught their 'proper' sex roles. In the next extract Judy Samuel looks at recent research on the way females are portrayed in science textbooks.

Reading 14   Messages in science textbooks

A careful and detailed study of the gender of people in illustrations in some current physics books has been carried out by Geoffrey Walford (1980). His survey shows that in the *Exploring Physics* series by Tom Duncan there is an overall bias in the illustrations of about four to one in favour of male characters. There are even fewer females in most of the other books examined in the survey. Analysis of the lavish and colourfully illustrated chemistry book we use with third-, fourth- and fifth-year pupils (Groves and Mansfield, 1981) gave an almost identical ratio of four illustrations showing men for every one showing a woman. Walford further comments that many of the illustrations featuring women show 'women pushing prams, a woman floating on the Dead Sea, girls blowing bubbles, women cooking, women as radiographers, nurses or patients, women used as sex symbols, women looking amazed or frightened, or simply women doing "silly" things'.

> (Judy Samuel, 'Science', in *Sexism in the Secondary Curriculum*, Janie Whyld (ed.), London, Harper and Row, 1983, p. 141)

The message here obviously is that science is for boys rather than girls, but not only are children influenced by such images, so too are teachers, as Judy Samuel further points out.

Reading 15   Teachers and textbooks

I feel that in some respects it is very difficult for men physics and chemistry teachers not to discriminate against girls in their classes, even when they are aware of the possibility of this and make a conscious decision not to do so. For example, a great many physics and chemistry textbooks (especially those intended for either younger or less able pupils) refer to the student exclusively as 'he' and reinforce the masculinity of the subject through the pictures they use. In these circumstances it is hardly surprising that many male teachers use these same masculine terms uncritically. A few examples will illustrate how the message is conveyed to both the teacher and the pupils.

1 The Nuffield chemistry O level handbook (intended for teachers) has eleven photographs of students: eight of boys doing some of the most difficult experiments in the book, one of girls doing a simple experiment, one of boys watching a demonstration and one of boys and girls watching a film. Both the teachers shown are men.

2 McDuell, a modern book for pupils studying CSE chemistry, has a brightly coloured photograph on the front cover of a boy doing an experiment, and a girl standing behind him recording the results.

(Judy Samuel, 'Feminism and science teaching: some classroom observations', in *The Missing Half: Girls and Science Education*, A. Kelly (ed.), Manchester University Press, 1981, pp. 252–3)

Discussion questions

1 Try to obtain some science textbooks at your school and carry out a content analysis of the way girls are represented in them.
2 Some sociologists argue that the hidden curriculum is just as important in socializing and educating children as the official curriculum. Discuss.

Religion and the sociology of knowledge

Durkheim was one of the first sociologists to examine the role of religion in the production of human knowledge. This tradition has been continued by Berger and Luckmann, who claim that the sociology of knowledge and the sociology of religion are inextricably linked.

Reading 16   The sociology of knowledge and the sociology of religion

Our understanding of the sociology of knowledge leads to the conclusion that the sociologies of language and religion cannot be considered peripheral specialities of little interest to sociological theory as such, but have essential contributions to make to it. This insight is not new. Durkheim and his school had it, but it was lost for a variety of theoretically irrelevant reasons. We hope we have made it clear that the sociology of knowledge presupposes a sociology of language and a sociology of knowledge without a sociology of religion is impossible (and vice versa).

(P. Berger and T. Luckmann, *The Social Construction of Reality*, Hanmondsworth, Penguin, 1967, p. 207)

The importance of religion to Berger and Luckmann is that it provides a way of giving meaning to the world and provides answers to ultimate questions, as Stephen Mennell points out in the following extract.

Reading 17   The importance of religion

Much is explained by the fact that both Luckmann and Berger are sociologists of religion (Luckmann 1967; Berger 1973). Berger in particular has been concerned to establish the centrality of religion as an institution even in modern society. Using a very broad definition of religion, he argues that religion is the means by which a 'sacred cosmos', a 'sacred canopy', is established. This is coextensive with the 'nomos', the meaningful order and core values of a society, and religion thus provides a man with an ultimate shield against anomie. In short, religion always plays an important part in world building, and is 'the audacious attempt to conceive of the entire universe as being humanly significant'.

(Stephen Mennell, *Sociological Theory: Uses and Unities*, New York, Praeger, 1974, p. 51)

The definition of religion used by Berger and Luckmann is known as an *inclusive definition*. This means that, unlike some sociologists who see religion in its institutional form, Berger and Luckmann understand it in a much broader sense, as Peter Berger explains in the following extract.

Reading 18   The inclusive definition of religion

It is important to understand that what Durkheim means by religion is considerably more than what most people understand by this term. Sociologists have differed as to the manner in which religion is to be defined for their purposes. Most sociologists continue to follow a narrower definition of religion, one that is closer to common usage, in which religion refers only to those ultimate interpretations of life that contain a belief in God, or gods or other supernatural entities. Thus, under a Durkheimian definition of religion, such overarching frameworks for human life as Marxism, Nationalism or the ethic of sexual liberation would be called 'religion', just as Christianity or Judaism would be, because all of these fulfil essentially similar social functions. Under a more conventional definition of religion, of course, the former group of belief systems would be called by some other term to distinguish them from such religions, in the narrower sense, as the Christian or Jewish ones.

(P. Berger and B. Berger, *Sociology: A Biographical Account*, Harmordsworth, Penguin, 1976, p. 380)

Although both Berger and Luckmann adhere to an inclusive definition of religion they do differ in terms of how far they would go in defining a system of beliefs as religious. Luckmann, for example, in his book *The Invisible Religion* (1967) describes any system of beliefs which tries to explain our place in the cosmos as religious. This would include such belief systems as science and Marxism. P. Berger, however, does not go as far as this, and in the next extract he explains why.

Reading 19   Science – a religion?

I question the utility of a definition that equates religion with the human *tout court*. It is one thing to point up the anthropological foundations of religion in the human capacity for self transcendence, quite another to equate the two. There are, after all, modes of self transcendence and concomitant symbolic universes that are vastly different from each other, whatever the identity of their anthropological origins. Thus, little is gained, in my opinion, by calling, say, modern science a form of religion.

(Peter Berger, *The Social Reality of Religion*, Harmondsworth, Penguin, 1969, p. 180)

In *The Social Reality of Religion*, Peter Berger attempts to outline the main characteristics of religion and its changing role in society. For Berger, one of its most important features is that it provides society with a *theodicy*, a definition of which is provided by Roy Wallis in the next extract.

Reading 20   Explanation of a theodicy

The need to endow suffering and evil with moral meaning and purpose is an issue addressed in various ways by religions. Christianity offers various resolutions to the problem of theodicy: misfortune may be a means of testing faith or of returning the thoughts of a backslider to God; it may be an attack by the Devil; the visiting of iniquity to the seventh generation; or insignificant in comparison to eternal glories and rewards. Non-Christian resolutions to the problem of theodicy may cite witchcraft, inauspicious astrological formations, or the act of evil spirits as the cause. The Hindu and Buddhist doctrine of Karma explains present misfortune and suffering by reference to deeds performed in a previous life (i.e. misfortune is only apparently undeserved).

(R. Wallis in *The Macmillan Student Encyclopedia of Sociology*, M. Mann (ed.), London, Macmillan, 1984, p. 395)

According to Berger, the plausibility structure of classical Western Christianity has been eroded by the process of secularization. This was partly a result of the disenchantment of the Western world and the increasingly rational outlook it promoted. Nevertheless, according to Berger, this does not mean that religion is any less important today but that we now have religious pluralism in which a variety of religious groups compete with one another in the market for ideas about ultimate meaning. In the following extract we can see how Berger uses the market analogy.

Reading 21   The market for religious ideas

The pluralistic situation is above all, a market situation. In it, the religious traditions become consumer commodities. And at any rate a good deal of religious activity in this situation comes to be dominated by the logic of market economics.

(Berger, *The Social Reality of Religion*, p. 142)

Although Berger and Luckmann argue that religion has lost much of its institutional importance through the process of secularization, they claim that it still plays an important part in people's lives in its privatized form. Thus religion has undergone a process of *transformation* which involves the individual finding his or her own salvation with the help of the new personalized religions. In the following extract Roy Wallis describes how scientology claims to do this.

Reading 22   Scientology

Scientology offered a wide range of practices designed to enable an individual to achieve his full potential as a human being and ultimately as a spiritual entity. It claimed to be able to eliminate psychosomatic and psychological illness and their effects, to increase intelligence, and to improve greatly the individual's functioning in interpersonal relations and in his career. In addition, it promised the committed follower the means to recover extraordinary spiritual powers . . . such as the ability to see and hear things at a great distance, to be able to manipulate objects by purely mental means, to gain knowledge of previous lives, and to be able to dominate other beings. Scientology claims to be able to produce these results on the basis of training and 'auditing', a technique of counselling and mental and spiritual exercises. Training and auditing are provided at varying fees, but advancement in scientology will normally cost several thousand pounds, or alternatively one may become a full time worker for the movement, receiving training and auditing free or at low cost in return for working at generally rather poor rates of pay.

(Roy Wallis, 'The Sociology of the New Religions', in *Social Studies Review*, vol. 1, no. 1, September 1985, p. 4)

Bryan Wilson does not interpret the process of secularization in the same way as Berger and Luckmann and claims that it is leading to a potentially dangerous situation. He suggests that in the past we lived in *communities* in which religion was a source of social knowledge and provided common values by which to live our lives and it therefore contributed to the stability of the community. According to Wilson, we now live in a *rational society* which provides us with no common moral standards, and he claims that this can have a harmful effect on society, as he explains in the next extract.

Reading 23   The moral community and the rational society

The balance of the communal order was struck in a personalised world that was part of a moral universe. The individual was involved in a society in which moral judgements were the basis of decisions, or purported to be so. To say this, is not to say that those judgements were right, but only to indicate that this was the style of decision making. The world was suffused with values, and the values often occluded the facts. In a societal system, such judgements cease to have relevance; custom, which was the code in which many such values were enshrined and given partial expression, falls into decay. It no longer serves as a buffer zone, protecting men from the abrasiveness of the operation of the law; no longer operates to communicate a sense of rectitude and to state the terms in which men may enjoy the goodwill (or the ill-will) of their fellows. The society is underwritten by no such values, but by empirical facts and their rational coordination: what good is custom when we have discovered a faster, cheaper, quicker, way to go about things?

(B. Wilson, *Religion in Sociological Perspective*, Oxford University Press, 1982, p. 162)

Discussion questions

1 Why do Berger and Luckmann consider religion to be such an important part of society?
2 How does the definition of religion used by Berger and Luckmann differ from other sociological definitions of religion?
3 In what way does religion differ from other belief systems?
4 In what ways do the explanations of misfortune in secular society differ from religious ones?
5 How is religion 'sold' in a society characterized by religious pluralism? Look at the way some of the new religions market themselves.
6 If there is nothing to replace religion as a source of social knowlege and common values, what consequences might this have for society?

Further reading

Abercrombie, N., *Class, Structure and Knowledge: Problems in the Sociology of Knowledge*, Oxford, Blackwell, 1980.
   A Marxist explanation of the origins of knowledge and ideas in society. In particular Abercrombie explains the relationship between the economic base and the superstructure.

Beck, J., Jenks, C., Keddie, N., and Young, M. F. D., *Worlds Apart: Readings for a Sociology of Education*, London, Collier-Macmillan, 1976.
   This book contains a number of interesting articles on the sociology of educntion, in particular those which illustrate how concepts such as 'ability', 'skill' and 'valid knowledge' can vary from society to society.

Berger, P., and Luckmann, T., *The Social Construction of Reality*: *A Treatise on the Sociology of Knowledge*, Harmondsworth, Penguin, 1976.
   In this book Berger and Luckmann analyse the origins of commonsense knowledge in society and how it takes on the status of objective reality. A classic in the field of the sociology of knowledge.

Frazer J. G., *The Golden Bough: A Study in Magic and Religion*, London, Macmillan, 1974.
   First published in 1922 this book raises one of the fundamental questions in the sociology of knowledge: how we make sense of the world around us. Frazer claims that the belief systems of magic, religion and science are all attempts to understand the world and therefore have more in common than we may at first think.

Glover, D., and Strawbridge, S., *The Sociology of Knowledge*, Ormskirk, Causeway Press, 1985.
   A good general introduction to the sociology of knowledge for the A-level student, containing clear and relevant examples.

Hamilton, P., *Knowledge and Social Structure*, London, Routledge and Kegan Paul, 1974.
This is a comprehensive study which examines the origins and development of the sociology of knowledge. The text is difficult in places, however, and I recommend it only to the keenest of students.

Kuhn, T., *The Structure of Scientific Revolutions*, University of Chicago Press, 1970.
In this pioneering book Kuhn questions the traditional notion of science as an objective progression towards the truth.

Richards, S., *Philosophy and Sociology of Science: an Introduction*, Oxford, Blackwell, 1983.
A good summary of and introduction to theories in the sociology of science.

'Society Today: knowledge' in *New Society*, 3, March 1983.
This introductory article presents the main issues in the sociology of knowledge in a concise and accessible way.

Slattery, M., *Official Statistics*, London, Tavistock Publications, 1985.
An excellent discussion on the production and use of official and other statistics, but without any of the complicated number crunching.

Whyld, J. (ed.), *Sexism in the Secondary Curriculum*, London, Harper and Row, 1983.
Contributions by a number of researchers on sexism in both the official and hidden curriculum.

Young, M. F. D. (ed.), *Knowledge and Control: New Directions in the Sociology of Education*, London, Collier-Macmillan, 1971.
A seminal work containing a number of essays on the new sociology of education which examine educational issues from the perspective of the sociology of knowledge.

Index